Canadian Daily Phonics
Grade 2

About this book:
These 32 weekly lessons will provide a strong phonetic background for Grade Two students. The lessons cover a wide range of skills needed to develop strong reading skills. The skills taught and reinforced are initial, medial and final consonants; long and short vowels; syllabication; blends; digraphs; hard and soft 'c' and 'g'; double vowel combinations; silent consonants; contractions; prefixes and suffixes.

Written by Ruth Solski
Illustrated by On The Mark Press

About the author:
Ruth Solski has been an educator for over 30 years and is the founder of S&S Learning Materials, now On The Mark Press. As a writer, she strives to provide teachers with a useful tool to bring the joy of learning to many children. She has always believed that practise makes perfection.

Copyright © On The Mark Press 2017

This publication may be reproduced under licence from Access Copyright, or with the express written permission of On The Mark Press, or as permitted by law. All rights are otherwise reserved, and no part of this publication may be reproduced, stored in a retrieval system, or transmitted in any form or by any means, electronic, mechanical, photocopying, scanning, recording or otherwise, except as specifically authorized.

All Rights Reserved.

Printed in Canada.

Published in Canada by:
On The Mark Press
Belleville, ON
www.onthemarkpress.com

Funded by the Government of Canada

SSR1141 ISBN: 9781771586870 © On The Mark Press

Canadian Daily Phonics

Grade Two

Table of Contents

Week 1 7	Week 19 115
Week 2 13	Week 20 121
Week 3 19	Week 21 127
Week 4 25	Week 22 133
Week 5 31	Week 23 139
Week 6 37	Week 24 145
Week 7 43	Week 25 151
Week 8 49	Week 26 157
Week 9 55	Week 27 163
Week 10 61	Week 28 169
Week 11 67	Week 29 175
Week 12 73	Week 30 181
Week 13 79	Week 31 187
Week 14 85	Week 32 193
Week 15 91	Student Assessment Sheet 199
Week 16 97	Student Phonic Award 200
Week 17 103	
Week 18 109	

Canadian Daily Phonics
Sequential Development of Skills

Week 1: Review Upper and Lower Case Letters of the Alphabet
Week 2: Initial Consonant Review
Week 3: Final Consonant Review
Week 4: Initial and Final Consonants
Week 5: Single Medial Consonants; Middle and Final Double Consonants
Week 6: Short Vowel Sounds 'Aa' and 'Ii'
Week 7: Recognition of the Short Vowel 'Uu'
Week 8: Introduction of Short Vowel 'Oo'; Review of Short Vowels 'a,e,i,u'
Week 9: Review of Short Vowels 'a,e,i,o,u'
Week 10: Introduction of Long Vowel Sounds - a,e,i,o,u
Week 11: Long and Short Vowels in Compound Words
Week 12: Syllabication in Regular and Compound Words
Week 13: Long and Short Vowel Sounds of 'Yy'
Week 14: Initial Consonant Blends: sl, st, sk, sp, sm, sn, sw
Week 15: Initial Consonant Blends: cl, bl, fl, gl, pl, sl
Week 16: Initial Consonant Blends: br, cr, dr, fr, gr, pr, tr
Week 17: Inital and Final Digraphs: sh, ch, wh, th
Week 18: Final Digraphs: ph, gh, ck, ng
Week 19: 'R' Controlled Vowels: ar, er, ir, or, ur
Week 20: Hard and Soft 'Cc' and 'Gg'
Week 21: Regular Double Vowels 'ai' and 'ay'
Week 22: Long 'e' Vowel Digraphs: 'ee, ea'
Week 23: Long 'i' Digraphs: igh, ie
Week 24: Vowel Digraphs 'oa, oe, ow, ue, ew'
Week 25: Vowel Digraph, Review
Week 26: Diphthongs 'ou, ow, oi, oy'
Week 27: The Two Sounds Made by 'oo'
Week 28: Silent Consonants 'k, w, l, b'
Week 29: Contractions
Week 30: Irregular Double Vowels: oo, ea, oi, oy, ow
Week 31: Prefixes 're, un, dis'
Week 32: Suffixes 's, es, ed, ing'

How to Use This Book

The Canadian Phonics Book for Grade 2 contains thirty-two weekly lesson plans for the various phonetic skills required by Grade 2 students to develop strong reading skills. The skills taught and reinforced are initial, medial and final consonants; long and short vowels; syllabication; blends; digraphs; hard and soft 'c' and 'g'; double vowel combinations; silent consonants; contractions; prefixes and suffixes. Each week contains Weekly Lesson Plans, Daily Worksheets and a Weekly Test.

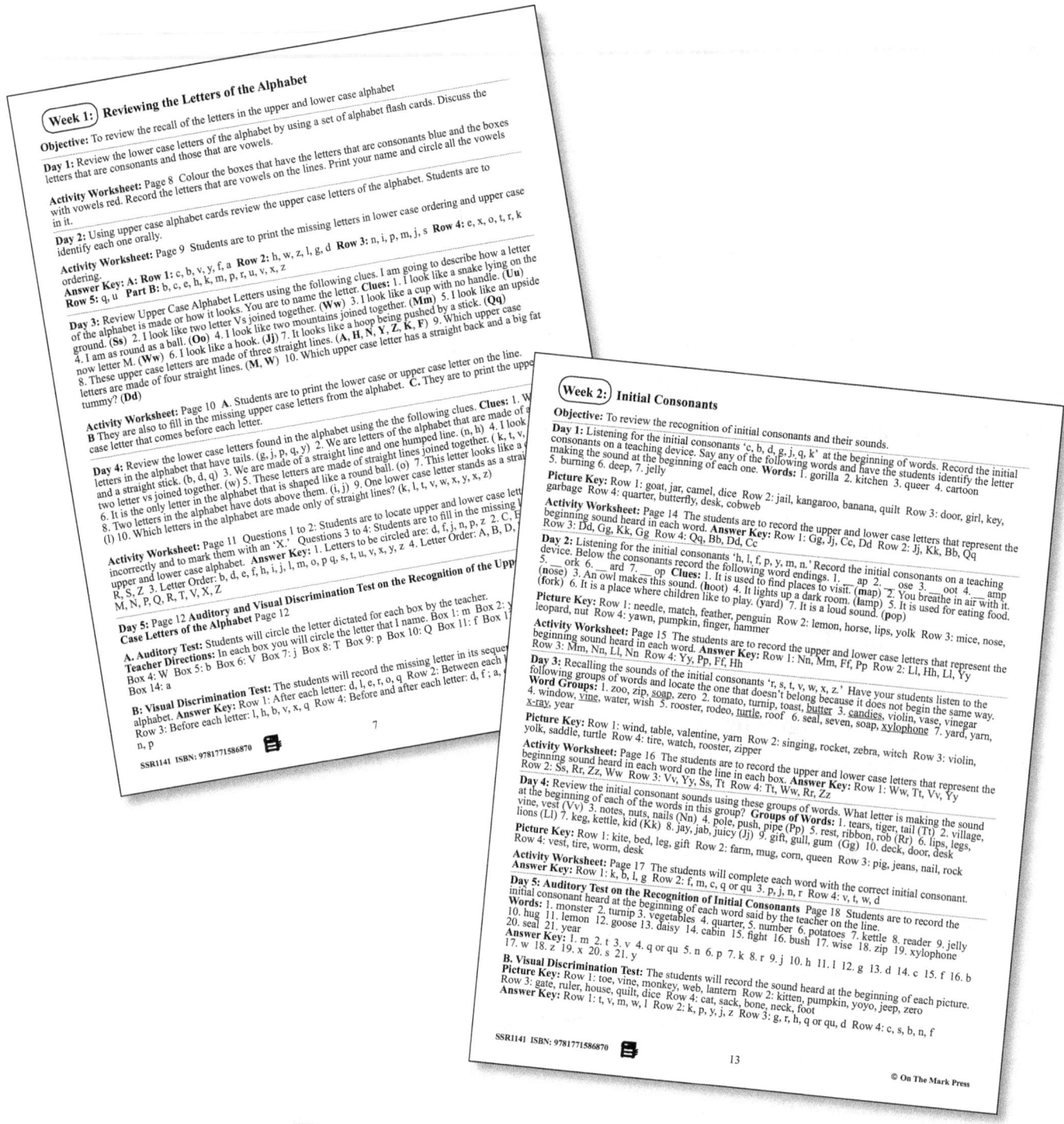

Student Worksheets

Weekly Tests

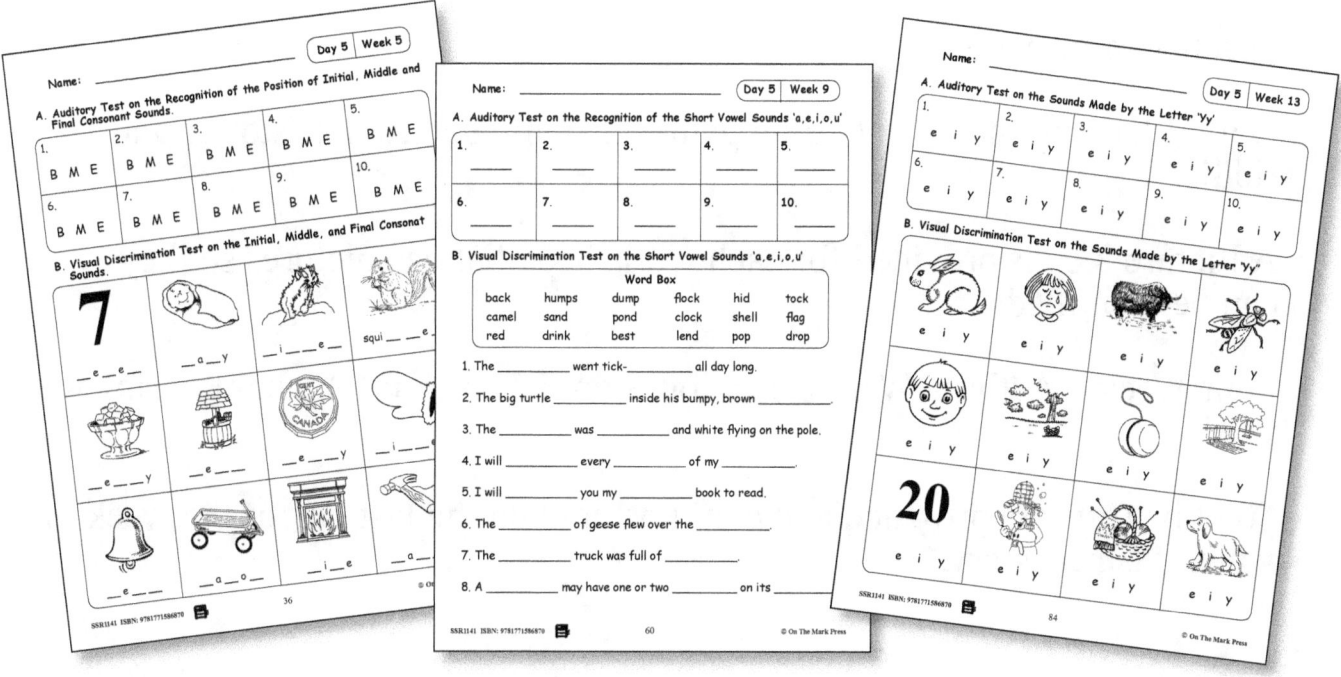

Ways to Use the Weekly Plans

The teaching plans and activity sheets could be used with students in the following ways:

- on a weekly basis with a class or group of students

    or

- the ideas and worksheets could be used to suit students' needs

    or

- they could be used for teaching ideas

    or

- to reinforce individual students' phonetic skills during home study.

Each weekly plan contains an :

- Objective

- Teacher Information

- Daily Planning Ideas containing games, listening activities, stories and riddles.

- A Picture Key is provided for each worksheet that has pictures so they can be identified.

- Four Weekly Activity Worksheets focus on the concept(s) taught during the week.

- Weekly Tests are provided and could be held on the last day of the week or when it is necessary.

Week 1: Reviewing the Letters of the Alphabet

Objective: To review the recall of the letters in the upper and lower case alphabet

Day 1: Review the lower case letters of the alphabet by using a set of alphabet flash cards. Discuss the letters that are consonants and those that are vowels.

Activity Worksheet: Page 8 Colour the boxes that have the letters that are consonants blue and the boxes with vowels red. Record the letters that are vowels on the lines. Print your name and circle all the vowels in it.

Day 2: Using upper case alphabet cards review the upper case letters of the alphabet. Students are to identify each one orally.

Activity Worksheet: Page 9 Students are to print the missing letters in lower case ordering and upper case ordering.
Answer Key: A: Row 1: c, b, v, y, f, a **Row 2:** h, w, z, l, g, d **Row 3:** n, i, p, m, j, s **Row 4:** e, x, o, t, r, k **Row 5:** q, u **Part B:** b, c, e, h, k, m, p, r, u, v, x, z

Day 3: Review Upper Case Alphabet Letters using the following clues. I am going to describe how a letter of the alphabet is made or how it looks. You are to name the letter. **Clues:** 1. I look like a snake lying on the ground. (**Ss**) 2. I look like two letter Vs joined together. (**Ww**) 3. I look like a cup with no handle. (**Uu**) 4. I am as round as a ball. (**Oo**) 4. I look like two mountains joined together. (**Mm**) 5. I look like an upside now letter M. (**Ww**) 6. I look like a hook. (**Jj**) 7. It looks like a hoop being pushed by a stick. (**Qq**) 8. These upper case letters are made of three straight lines. (**A, H, N, Y, Z, K, F**) 9. Which upper case letters are made of four straight lines. (**M, W**) 10. Which upper case letter has a straight back and a big fat tummy? (**Dd**)

Activity Worksheet: Page 10 **A.** Students are to print the lower case or upper case letter on the line. **B** They are also to fill in the missing upper case letters from the alphabet. **C.** They are to print the upper case letter that comes before each letter.

Day 4: Review the lower case letters found in the alphabet using the the following clues. **Clues:** 1. We are letters in the alphabet that have tails. (g, j, p, q, y) 2. We are letters of the alphabet that are made of a ball and a straight stick. (b, d, q) 3. We are made of a straight line and one humped line. (n, h) 4. I look like two letter vs joined together. (w) 5. These letters are made of straight lines joined together. (k, t, v, w, x, z) 6. It is the only letter in the alphabet that is shaped like a round ball. (o) 7. This letter looks like a chair. (h) 8. Two letters in the alphabet have dots above them. (i, j) 9. One lower case letter stands as a straight stick (l) 10. Which letters in the alphabet are made only of straight lines? (k, l, t, v, w, x, y, x, z)

Activity Worksheet: Page 11 Questions 1 to 2: Students are to locate upper and lower case letters made incorrectly and to mark them with an 'X.' Questions 3 to 4: Students are to fill in the missing letters in the upper and lower case alphabet. **Answer Key:** 1. Letters to be circled are: d, f, j, n, p, z 2. C, E, G, J, L, P, R, S, Z 3. Letter Order: b, d, e, f, h, i, j, l, m, o, p q, s, t, u, v, x, y, z 4. Letter Order: A, B, D, E, G, H, J, K, M, N, P, Q, R, T, V, X, Z

Day 5: Page 12 **Auditory and Visual Discrimination Test on the Recognition of the Upper and Lower Case Letters of the Alphabet** Page 12

A. Auditory Test: Students will circle the letter dictated for each box by the teacher.
Teacher Directions: In each box you will circle the letter that I name. Box 1: m Box 2: y Box 3: N Box 4: W Box 5: b Box 6: V Box 7: j Box 8: T Box 9: p Box 10: Q Box 11: f Box 12: k Box 13: H Box 14: a

B: Visual Discrimination Test: The students will record the missing letter in its sequential order in the alphabet. **Answer Key:** Row 1: After each letter: d, l, e, r, o, q Row 2: Between each letter: i, o, d, s, q, t Row 3: Before each letter: l, h, b, v, x, q Row 4: Before and after each letter: d, f ; a, c ; f, h ; l, n; w, y; n, p

Name: _____   Day 1 | Week 1

The letters in the alphabet are used to make words

Each one has its own shape and size.

Some are consonants while others are vowels.

Colour all the boxes that have letters called **consonants** blue. Colour all the boxes that have **vowels** red.

a	b	c	d	e	f
g	h	i	j	k	l
m	n	o	p	q	r
s	t	u	v	w	x
y	z				

There are **five** letters that are **vowels** in the alphabet. Print their names on the lines.

1. _____ 2. _____ 3. _____ 4. _____ 5. _____

Print your first and last name on the line. Circle the vowels in it.

_____

Name: _____   Day 2 | Week 1

> The letters in the alphabet come in **two** sizes.
> They are **upper case** and **lower case**.
> **Upper case** letters are taller and are called **capital letters**.
> **Examples:** A, B, C, D, E
> **Lower case** letters are smaller and have different shapes.
> **Examples:** a, b, c, d, e

A. Each capital letter has a partner. Example: Bb
On each line print the capital letter's partner.

C ___	B ___	V ___	Y ___	F ___	A ___
H ___	W ___	Z ___	L ___	G ___	D ___
N ___	I ___	P ___	M ___	J ___	S ___
E ___	X ___	O ___	T ___	R ___	K ___
Q ___	U ___				

B. Print the missing lower case letters.

a ___ ___ d ___ f g ___ i j ___ l ___ n o ___ q ___
s t ___ ___ w ___ y ___

Name: _____   Day 3 | Week 1

Each letter of the alphabet has a partner.
One is tall while the other one is small.
Can you match each letter to its partner?

A. Print the **upper** or **lower** case partner for the following letters.

1. c ___   6. a ___   11. R ___   16. c ___
2. E ___   7. h ___   12. B ___   17. y ___
3. u ___   8. l ___   13. d ___   18. F ___
4. X ___   9. m ___   14. f ___   19. j ___
5. Q ___   10. p ___   15. G ___   20. K ___

B. Print the **upper case letter** that comes before each of the following letters.

1. ___ R   5. ___ B   9. ___ T   13. ___ Y
2. ___ W   6. ___ D   10. ___ F   14. ___ P
3. ___ Q   7. ___ H   11. ___ N   15. ___ R
4. ___ M   8. ___ K   12. ___ V   16. ___ Z

C. Print the **lower case** letter that comes **before** each of the following letters.

1. ___ C   5. ___ d   9. ___ p   13. ___ b
2. ___ g   6. ___ m   10. ___ x   14. ___ e
3. ___ t   7. ___ s   11. ___ f   15. ___ u
4. ___ w   8. ___ k   12. ___ h   16. ___ z

Name: _____ Day 4 | Week 1

 Letters of the alphabet must be made correctly. They have a certain size, shape and face in a certain direction.

1. Put an X on each lower case letter that is travelling the wrong way in the alphabet.

a	d	c	d	e	ɟ	g	h	i	ɿ
k	l	m	ᴎ	o	q	q	r	s	t
ʇ	u	v	w	x	y	ƨ			

2. Circle the upper case letters that are travelling the wrong way in the alphabet.

A	B	Ɔ	D	Ǝ	F	ә	H	I	ſ
K	˩	M	N	O	ꟼ	Q	Я	ƨ	T
U	V	W	X	Y	Ƨ				

3. Print the letters of the lower case alphabet in the correct order.

a __ c __ __ __ __ g __ __ __ k __ __ n __ __ __ __
r __ __ __ __ __ w __ __ __ __

4. Print the missing letters of the upper case alphabet in the correct order.

__ __ C __ __ F __ __ I __ __ L __ __ O __
__ __ S __ U __ W __ Y __

SSR1141 ISBN: 9781771586870   11   © On The Mark Press

Name: _____ Day 5 | Week 1

A. Auditory Test on the Recognition of the Upper and Lower Case Letters of the Alphabet.

1. r	2. g	3. M	4. A	5. p	6. w	7. e
m	j	N	V	b	v	c
n	y	v	w	q	y	j
8. A	9. b	10. O	11. h	12. l	13. E	14. o
K	d	Q	j	k	F	a
T	p	D	f	h	H	c

B. Visual Discrimination of the Upper and Lower Case Letters of the Alphabet

Row 1	Row 2	Row 3	Row 4
c ___	h ___ j	___ k	___ e ___
k ___	n ___ p	___ i	___ b ___
d ___	c ___ e	___ c	___ g ___
q ___	r ___ t	___ w	___ m ___
n ___	p ___ r	___ y	___ x ___
p ___	s ___ u	___ r	___ o ___

Week 2: **Initial Consonants**

Objective: To review the recognition of initial consonants and their sounds.

Day 1: Listening for the initial consonants 'c, b, d, g, j, q, k' at the beginning of words. Record the initial consonants on a teaching device. Say any of the following words and have the students identify the letter making the sound at the beginning of each one. **Words:** 1. gorilla 2. kitchen 3. queer 4. cartoon 5. burning 6. deep, 7. jelly

Picture Key: Row 1: goat, jar, camel, dice Row 2: jail, kangaroo, banana, quilt Row 3: door, girl, key, garbage Row 4: quarter, butterfly, desk, cobweb

Activity Worksheet: Page 14 The students are to record the upper and lower case letters that represent the beginning sound heard in each word. **Answer Key:** Row 1: Gg, Jj, Cc, Dd Row 2: Jj, Kk, Bb, Qq Row 3: Dd, Gg, Kk, Gg Row 4: Qq, Bb, Dd, Cc

Day 2: Listening for the initial consonants 'h, l, f, p, y, m, n.' Record the initial consonants on a teaching device. Below the consonants record the following word endings. 1. __ap 2. __ose 3. __oot 4. __amp 5. __ork 6. __ard 7. __op **Clues:** 1. It is used to find places to visit. (**m**ap) 2. You breathe in air with it. (**n**ose) 3. An owl makes this sound. (**h**oot) 4. It lights up a dark room. (**l**amp) 5. It is used for eating food. (**f**ork) 6. It is a place where children like to play. (**y**ard) 7. It is a loud sound. (**p**op)

Picture Key: Row 1: needle, match, feather, penguin Row 2: lemon, horse, lips, yolk Row 3: mice, nose, leopard, nut Row 4: yawn, pumpkin, finger, hammer

Activity Worksheet: Page 15 The students are to record the upper and lower case letters that represent the beginning sound heard in each word. **Answer Key:** Row 1: Nn, Mm, Ff, Pp Row 2: Ll, Hh, Ll, Yy Row 3: Mm, Nn, Ll, Nn Row 4: Yy, Pp, Ff, Hh

Day 3: Recalling the sounds of the initial consonants 'r, s, t, v, w, x, z.' Have your students listen to the following groups of words and locate the one that doesn't belong because it does not begin the same way. **Word Groups:** 1. zoo, zip, soap, zero 2. tomato, turnip, toast, butter 3. candies, violin, vase, vinegar 4. window, vine, water, wish 5. rooster, rodeo, turtle, roof 6. seal, seven, soap, xylophone 7. yard, yarn, x-ray, year

Picture Key: Row 1: wind, table, valentine, yarn Row 2: singing, rocket, zebra, witch Row 3: violin, yolk, saddle, turtle Row 4: tire, watch, rooster, zipper

Activity Worksheet: Page 16 The students are to record the upper and lower case letters that represent the beginning sound heard in each word on the line in each box. **Answer Key:** Row 1: Ww, Tt, Vv, Yy Row 2: Ss, Rr, Zz, Ww Row 3: Vv, Yy, Ss, Tt Row 4: Tt, Ww, Rr, Zz

Day 4: Review the initial consonant sounds using these groups of words. What letter is making the sound at the beginning of each of the words in this group? **Groups of Words:** 1. tears, tiger, tail (Tt) 2. village, vine, vest (Vv) 3. notes, nuts, nails (Nn) 4. pole, push, pipe (Pp) 5. rest, ribbon, rob (Rr) 6. lips, legs, lions (Ll) 7. keg, kettle, kid (Kk) 8. jay, jab, juicy (Jj) 9. gift, gull, gum (Gg) 10. deck, door, desk

Picture Key: Row 1: kite, bed, leg, gift Row 2: farm, mug, corn, queen Row 3: pig, jeans, nail, rock Row 4: vest, tire, worm, desk

Activity Worksheet: Page 17 The students will complete each word with the correct initial consonant. **Answer Key:** Row 1: k, b, l, g Row 2: f, m, c, q or qu 3. p, j, n, r Row 4: v, t, w, d

Day 5: Auditory Test on the Recognition of Initial Consonants Page 18 Students are to record the initial consonant heard at the beginning of each word said by the teacher on the line.
Words: 1. monster 2. turnip 3. vegetables 4. quarter, 5. number 6. potatoes 7. kettle 8. reader 9. jelly 10. hug 11. lemon 12. goose 13. daisy 14. cabin 15. fight 16. bush 17. wise 18. zip 19. xylophone 20. seal 21. year
Answer Key: 1. m 2. t 3. v 4. q or qu 5. n 6. p 7. k 8. r 9. j 10. h 11. l 12. g 13. d 14. c 15. f 16. b 17. w 18. z 19. x 20. s 21. y

B. Visual Discrimination Test: The students will record the sound heard at the beginning of each picture.
Picture Key: Row 1: toe, vine, monkey, web, lantern Row 2: kitten, pumpkin, yoyo, jeep, zero Row 3: gate, ruler, house, quilt, dice Row 4: cat, sack, bone, neck, foot
Answer Key: Row 1: t, v, m, w, l Row 2: k, p, y, j, z Row 3: g, r, h, q or qu, d Row 4: c, s, b, n, f

Name: _____ Day 1 | Week 2

Each initial consonant makes its **own sound** at the **beginning** of words.

Listen for and print the **upper case** and **lower case** letter that makes the beginning sound for each picture on the line under each one.

Cc   Bb   Dd   Gg   Jj   Qq   Kk

Name: _____ Day 2 | Week 2

Each initial consonant makes its **own sound** at the **beginning** of words.

Listen for and print the **upper case** and **lower case** letter that makes the beginning sound for each picture on the line below each one.

Hh   Ll   Ff   Pp   Yy   Mm   Nn

Name: _____   Day 3 | Week 2

Each initial consonant makes its **own sound** at the **beginning** of words.

Listen for and print the **upper case** and **lower case** letter that makes the beginning sound for each picture on the line below each one.

    Rr   Ss   Tt   Vv   Ww   Xx   Zz

Name: _____   Day 4 | Week 2

How well do you know the initial consonants?
Record the letter that makes the beginning sound heard in each picture and its word.

___ite	___ed	___eg	___ift
___arm	___ug	___orn	___ueen
___ig	___eans	___ail	___ock
___est	___ire	___orm	___esk

Name: _____ Day 5 | Week 2

A. Auditory Test on the Recognition of the Initial Consonants and Their Sounds

1. ___	2. ___	3. ___	4. ___	5. ___	6. ___	7. ___
8. ___	9. ___	10. ___	11. ___	12. ___	13. ___	14. ___
15. ___	16. ___	17. ___	18. ___	19. ___	20. ___	21. ___

B. Visual Discrimination Test on the Initial Consonants and Their Sounds

Week 3: Final Consonants

Objective: To review the recognition of all final consonants and their sounds. Final consonants are b, d, f, g, k, l, m, n, p, r, s, t, x, z.

Day 1: Record the final consonants b, d, f, g, k, l, m on a chart. Explain to your students that many words end with letters of the alphabet and they are called final consonants. Tell them to listen to the end of each word that you say and then locate the final sound on the chart. **Words:** 1. muff 2. hard 3. stub 4. charm 5. fool 6. hum 7. tack 8. zoom 9. stiff 10. club

Picture Key: Row 1: ham, book, pool, pig Row 2: cab, leaf, toad, jam Row 3: nail, rink, dog, roof

Activity Worksheet: Page 20 The students are to record the initial and final consonants to complete each word that describes the picture. **Answer Key:** Row 1: h, m; b, k; p, l; p, g Row 2: c, b; l, f; t, d; j, m; Row 3: n, l; r, k; d, g; r, f

Day 2: Have the students listen carefully for any of the following final sounds: n, p, r, s, t, x, z that are printed on a chart. Explain they are to listen to the ending of each word that you are going to say. The students are to locate the final consonant sound on the chart. **Words:** 1. moon 2. buzz 3. fear 4. hiss 5. rabbit 6. hoop 7. box 8. fuzz 9. hammer 10. hump

Picture Key: Row 1: moon, lamp, deer, kiss Row 2: nut, fox, gas, bat Row 3: rain, pump, box, pot

Activity Worksheet: Page 21 The students are to record the initial and final consonants to complete each word that describes the picture. **Answer Key:** Row 1: m, n; l, p; d, r; l, s Row 2: n. t; f, x; g, s; b, t Row 3: r, n; p, p; b, x; p, t

Day 3: Review the initial and final consonants heard in words using the following riddles. **Riddles:** 1. I begin with 'r' and end with 't'. I am an animal that likes to hop. (rabbit) 2. I am a toy that looks like a circle and goes round and round a body. I begin with 'h' and end with 'p.' (hoop) 3. I melt when I am lit. I am in a candle. I begin with 'w' and end with 'x.' (wax) 4. You can sleep outside in me. I begin and end with the letter 't.' (tent) 5. It is a group of people who like to play music. The word begins with 'b' and ends with 'd.' (band) 6. I am part of a house. I begin with 'r' and end with 'f.' (roof) 7. I am a home for an insect. I am also used to catch my owner's food. I begin with 'w' and end with 'b.' (web) 8. I look like a frog but I never go in water. I like to live in a garden. I begin with 't' and end with 'd.' (toad)

Picture Key: Row 1: box, map, bus, rug Row 2: feet, cab, bear, log Row 3: jug, bib, hand, bank Row 4: jam, loaf, well, dog Row 5: pen, sink, van, bag

Activity Worksheet: Page 22 The students will print the initial and final consonants to complete each word to match each picture. **Answer Key:** Row 1: box, map, bus, rug Row 2: feet, cab, bear, leg Row 3: jug, bib, hand, bank Row 4: jam, loaf, well, dog Row 5: pen, sink, van, bag

Day 4: Review making new words by changing the initial and final consonants in words. Record the following groups of words on a chart. **Groups of Words:** 1. rod, rub, rob 2. bug, bun, mug 3. bug, bun, but 4. pops, pots, pods 5. pad, pat, pal 6. pail, paid, pain 7. pig, pin, pit 8. room, roof, root 9. bed, bet, beg Have individual students say each group of words.

Activity Worksheet: Page 23 Students are to use their word attack skills to discover the correct word to complete each sentence. **Answer Key:** 1. rob 2. mug 3. pods 4. pad 5. cab 6. pain 7. pig 8. root 9. beg 10. fib

Day 5: A. Auditory Test on the Recognition of Final Consonants Page 24 Students are to record the final consonant heard at the end of each word said by the teacher. On each line the students will record the final sound heard. **Words:** 1. trunk 2. wheel 3. cream 4. train, 5. camp 6. jar 7. pass 8. float 9. buzz 10. six 11. flag 12. bread 13. hoof 14. honk Answer Key: 1. k 2. l 3. m 4. n 5. p 6. r 7. s 8. t 9. z 10. x 11. g 12. d 13. f 14. k

B. Visual Discrimination Test: The students will record the sound heard at the end of each picture. **Picture Key:** Row 1: hook, pail, tub, deer, well Row 2: coat, dog, drum, pen, mat Row 3: roof, clam, glass, sand, star Row 4: sheep, ax, book, spoon, seal **Answer Key:** Row 1: k, l, b, r, l Row 2: t, g, m, n, t Row 3: f, m, s, d, r Row 4: p, x, k, n, l

Name: _____   Day 1 | Week 3

 Many words that we use begin and end with a consonant.

Examples: **bad, roof, rub, mug, mail, peck, ham**

Print the **initial** and **final** consonant heard at the beginning and ending of each picture on the lines to make the word.

__ a __	__ oo __	__ oo __	__ i __
__ a __	__ ea __	__ oa __	__ a __
__ ai __	__ in __	__ o __	__ oo __

Name: _____ Day 2 | Week 3

Many words that we use begin and end with a consonant
Examples:
    bun   hop   roar   mug   bus   cat   box   fuzz

Print the **initial** and **final** consonant heard at the **beginning**
and the **ending** of each picture on the lines to complete the word.

___ oo ___	___ am ___	___ ee ___	___ i s ___
___ u ___	___ o ___	___ a ___	___ a ___
___ ai ___	___ um ___	___ o ___	___ o ___

Name: _____ Day 3 | Week 3

It is important that you know the consonants that talk at the **beginning** and **ending** of words.

Record the initial and final consonant that is heard at the beginning and ending of each word.

			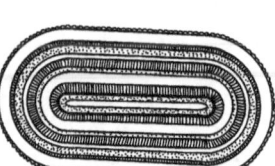
__ o __	__ a __	__ u __	__ u __
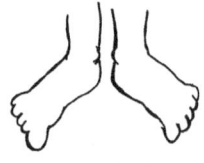			
__ e e __	__ a __	__ ea __	__ o __
		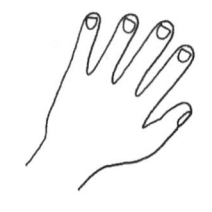	
__ u __	__ i __	__ an __	__ an __
	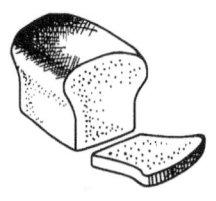		
__ a __	__ oa __	__ el __	__ o __

__ e __	__ in __	__ a __	__ g __

Name: _____ Day 4 | Week 3

A **new** word can be made by changing the **initial** or **final** consonant of a word.

Print the correct word in each of the following sentences.

1. I saw a man try to _____ a bank one day. (rod, rub, rob)

2. The boy likes to drink his milk using a big _____.
   (bug, bun, mug)

3. I helped my mom take the peas out of their _____.
   (pops, pods, pots)

4. The girl wrote a note to her mother on a little _____.
   (pat, pal, pad)

5. We drove to the airport in a big blue _____. (cap, can, cab)

6. The boy broke his leg and was in great _____.
   (pail, paid, pain)

7. The _____ lay in the mud in its pen. (pit, pin, pig)

8. A plant has a _____ that holds it in the ground.
   (roof, room, root)

9. The little dog likes to _____ for treats. (big, bug, beg)

10. The bad boy told the teacher a big _____. (rib, fib, bib)

Name: _____ Day 5 | Week 3

A. Auditory Test on the Recognition of the Final Consonants and Their Sounds.

1. ___	2. ___	3. ___	4. ___	5. ___	6. ___	7. ___
8. ___	9. ___	10. ___	11. ___	12. ___	13. ___	14. ___

B. Visual Discrimination Test on the Final Consonants and Their Sounds

SSR1141 ISBN: 9781771586870

© On The Mark Press

Week 4: Initial and Final Consonants

Objective: To review initial and final consonants and consonant substitution.

Day 1: Discuss initial consonant substitution with your students. Explain that many new words can be discovered by using the same word ending and changing the initial consonant. These groups of words are also called Word Families. Record on a chart the following word and word endings. **Example:** can, __an, __an, __an, __an, __an, __an, __an. There are seven words that rhyme with 'can.' All we have to do is to change the first sound. Record the missing letters. (d, f, m, p, r, t, v) Use other familiar word endings such as 'and, ad, at, ot' to make new words.

Picture Key: Row 1: tub, pot, bag, pup Row 2: jug, sun, nail, map, Row 3: fox, cab, log, lid Row 4: bib, bell, boat, six

Activity Worksheet: Page 26 Students are to record the intial consonant on the line that completes each word ending to match the picture. **Answer Key:** Row 1: tub, pot, bag, pup Row 2: jug, sun, nail, map 3. fox, cab, log, lid Row 4: bib, bell, boat, six

Day 2: Review changing the initial consonant sound at the beginning of word endings. On a chart record a word ending. Have the students skim through the alphabet to find letters that could be used to make new words. Example: ack: back, hack, Jack, lack, pack, rack, sack, tack Word Endings to be used: ump, amp, imp, ick, eck, uck, ock, ack

Activity Worksheet: Page 27 Students are to select the correct word and print it on the line in each sentence. **Answer Key:** 1. toad 2. kick 3. men 4. rain 5. test 6. zoom 7. puck 8. gum 9. cab 10. sand

Day 3: Review changing the final consonant sound heard at the end of words. On a chart record the following words in a list. **Words:** pot, cup, bat, dig, bed, lip Have your students read the list of words. Explain that they are to think of consonants that could be used to change the final sound to make new words. Example: pot, pod, pop

Picture Key: Row 1: web, lid, roof, leg Row 2: tent, book, tail, pin Row 3: fan, pool, jug, hand Row 4: jam, bug, cup, bus

Activity Worksheet: Page 28 Students are to print the correct word on the line to match the picture using a word beginning and a final consonant. **Answer Key:** Row 1: web, lid, roof, leg Row 2: tent, book, tail, pin Row 3: fan, pool, jug, hand Row 4: jam, bug, cup, bus

Day 4: Review how consonants can be changed at the ending of a word. Record the following word beginnings on a chart. 1. cu<u>b</u>, cu<u>d</u>, cu<u>p</u>, cu<u>t</u> 2. pa<u>d</u>, pa<u>d</u>, pa<u>n</u>, pa<u>t</u> 3. ca<u>b</u>, ca<u>n</u>, ca<u>p</u>, ca<u>r</u>, ca<u>t</u> Row 4. pi<u>g</u>, pi<u>n</u>, pi<u>t</u> 5. di<u>d</u>, di<u>g</u>, di<u>p</u> 6. ra<u>g</u>, ra<u>m</u>, ra<u>p</u>, ra<u>t</u>

Activity Worksheet: Page 29 Students are to select the correct word and print it on the line in each sentence. **Answer Key:** 1. pot 2. cub 3. rat 4. bud 5. lip 6. big 7. bat 8. rug 9. lit 10. cap

Day 5: Auditory Test on the Recognition of the Initial and Final Consonants and Their Sounds.
Page 30 The teacher will say a word and the students will record the initial and final consonants on the lines in each box. **Words:** 1. rob 2. send 3. hoof 4. goal 5. bunk 6. zoom 7. noon 8. meet 9. loop 10. kiss 11. fix 12. buzz **Answer Key:** 1. r, b 2. s, d 3. h, f 4. g, l 5. b, k 6. z, m 7. n, n 8. m, t 9. l, p 10. k, s 11. f, x 12. b, z

Visual Discrimination Test on the Initial and Final Consonants and Their Sounds: The students will record on the lines the initial and final consonants heard in each picture. Row 1: l, d; b, l; g, m; c, n; c, p Row 2: c, r; n, t; r, n; w, g; h, d Row 3: r, r; h, t; w, m; f, k; p, p Row 4: b, x; c, n; n, k; h, r; b, t

Picture Key: Row 1: lid, bell, gum, can, cap Row 2: car, net, run, wig, head Row 3: rooster, heart, worm, fork, pump Row 4: box, corn, neck, hair, boot

Name: _____ Day 1 | Week 4

You can discover and spell many words by changing the initial consonant at the beginning of many words.

Examples: bug, dug, hug, jug, lug, mug, rug, tug

Print the new word to match each picture. Use any of the following endings.

ix ell ow id ab ap un up ot ub ag ug ail ox og ib oat

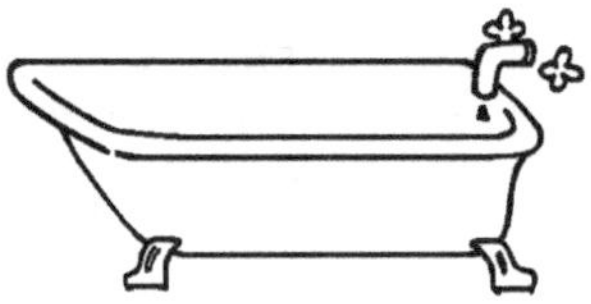

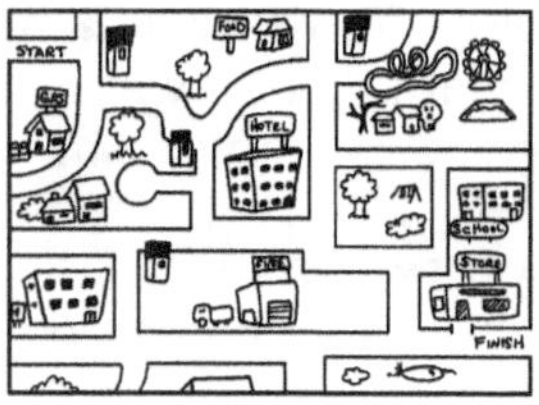

Name: _____   Day 2 | Week 4

 Many sounds can be changed at the beginning of word endings to make new words.

Examples: bell, dell, fell, sell, tell, well

Choose the correct **word** that completes each sentence. **Print** it on the line.

1. The little _____ hid under the bush so no one could see him.
   (load, road, toad)

2. The boys like to _____ the ball over the big field.
   (lick, kick, pick)

3. Some _____ worked to fill the big hole in the road.
   (den, hen, men)

4. The _____ made everything and everyone very wet.
   (main, rain, pain)

5. We had a big spelling _____ at school today.
   (test, pest, rest)

6. Race cars can _____ quickly around a track.
   (room, boom, zoom)

7. The hockey player hit the _____ and scored a goal.
   (luck, duck, puck)

8. Do not chew _____ at school.
   (hum, rum, gum)

9. We rode a _____ to the airport to catch a plane.
   (gab, cab, tab)

10. We played in the _____ at the beach all day.
    (band, land, sand)

Name: _____   Day 3 | Week 4

Many sounds can be changed at the **end** of word beginnings to make **new** words.

Examples: bud, bug, bun, bus, bu**t**

Print the new word to match each picture. Use any of the following word beginnings.

bu cu ja han ju poo boo fa pi tai boo ten le roo li we

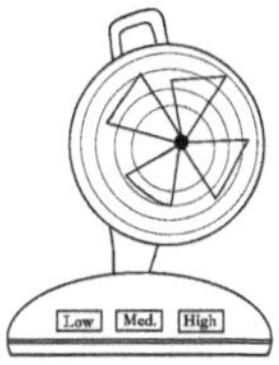

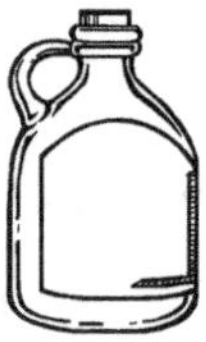

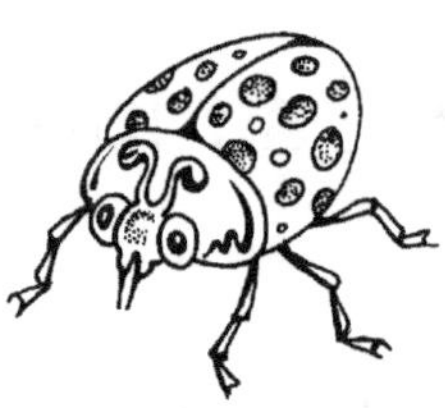

Name: _____   Day 4 | Week 4

Many sounds can be changed at the endings of words to make new words.

Examples: tab   tad   tag   tam   tan   tap

Choose the correct word that **completes** each sentence.
Print the word on the line.

1. My mother put the soup in a big _____ on the stove to get hot.
(pot, pod, pop)

2. The little bear _____ ate all the berries on the bush.
(cup, cut, cub)

3. The _____ ran under the steps to hide from the big black cat.
(rap, rat, ran)

4. The little _____ on the plant became a pretty, red flower.
(bug, bun, bud)

5. I bit my _____ when I fell and made it bleed.   (lit, lip, lid)

6. We climbed to the top of the _____ hill and slid down it.
(bit, big, bib)

7. A _____ likes to fly at night to catch bugs.   (bag, bad, bat)

8. The cat likes to sleep on the little brown _____ by the fire.
(run, rub, rug)

9. The boy _____ the candles on his birthday cake.   (lip, lit, lid)

10. The man wore a red and white _____ on his head.   (can, cat, cap)

Name: _____ Day 5 | Week 4

A. Auditory Test on the Recognition of the Initial and Final Consonants and Their Sounds.

1. __ __	2. __ __	3. __ __	4. __ __	5. __ __	6. __ __
7. __ __	8. __ __	9. __ __	10. __ __	11. __ __	12. __ __

B. Visual Discrimination Test on the Recognition of Initial and Final Consonants and Their Sounds.

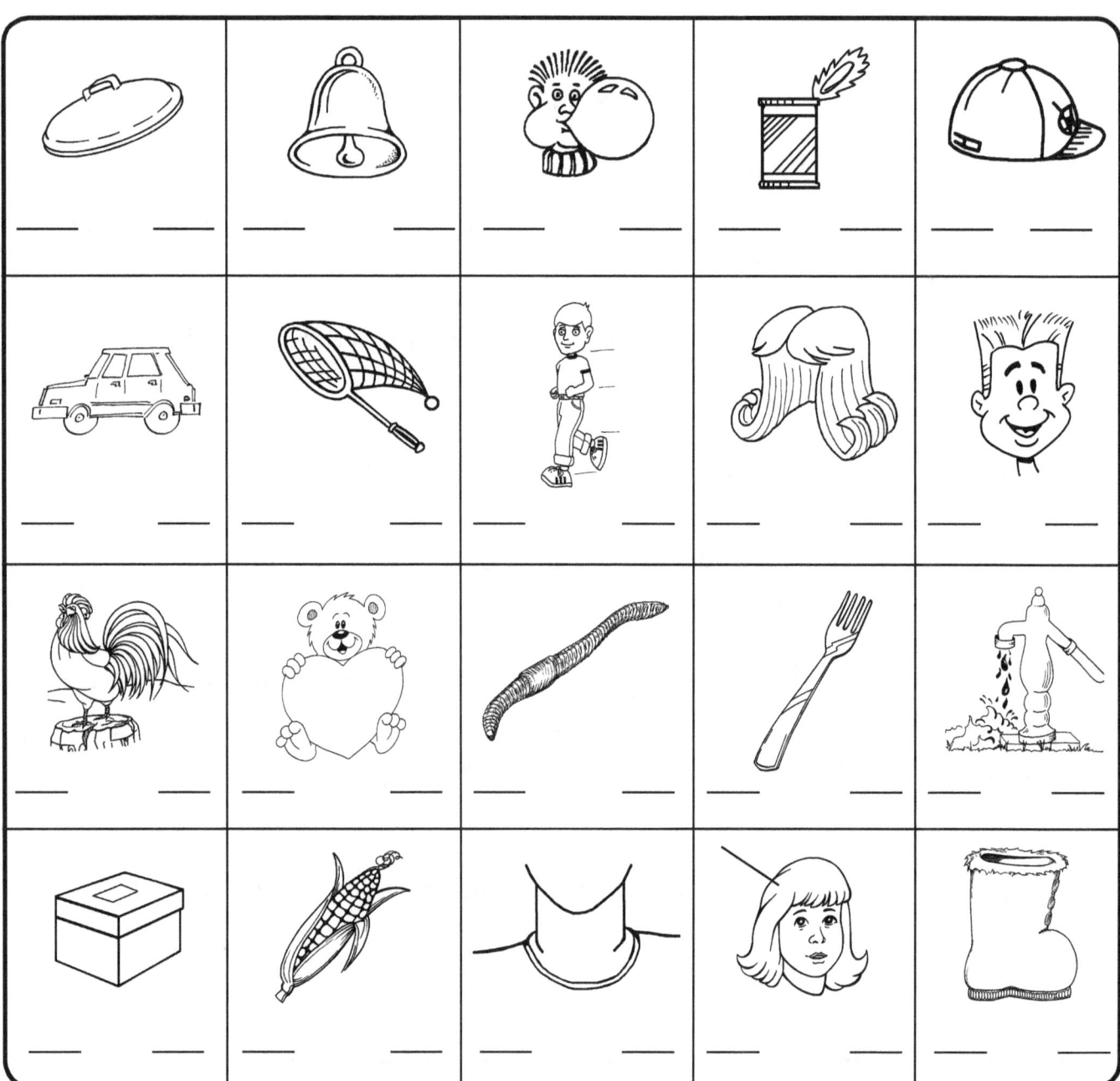

Week 5: **Single Medial Consonants; Middle and Final Double Consonants**

Objective: To make students aware that a single or a pair of double consonants may be found in the middle of a word or at the end of a word.

Day 1: Have students listen to the following groups of words for the consonant heard in the middle of each one. Explain that often a single consonant is heard in the middle of a word as well as at the beginning and ending. Have them listen for the consonant in the middle of the following words. **Words:** broken (k); cozy (z); city (t); gravel (v); story (r); cider (d); cover (v); pupil (p); stable (b); below (l); baker (k)

Picture Key: Row 1: wagon, camel, ruler, lady Row 2: seven, dragon, table, spider Row 3: robin, match, tiger, money Row 4: fire, baby, canoe, lemon

Activity Worksheet: Page 32 The students will complete each word with the correct single consonant to complete the name of each picture: **Answer Key:** Row 1: g, m, l, d Row 2: v, g, b, d Row 3: b, t, g, n Row 4: r, b, n, m

Day 2: On a chart print the following pairs of double consonants: bb, nn, rr, ll, mm, tt, dd, pp, ss, ff, zz. Explain to your students that two of the same consonants may appear in the middle or at the end of a word. In the middle of a word both consonants can be heard but at the end of a word both consonants make only one sound together. Say one of the following words: button, glass, summer, poppy, hill, grass, bunny, nibble, cottage. The students are to tell which pair of double consonants is heard and where they are located in the word.

Picture Key: Row 1: grass, ladder, zipper, well Row 2: glass, button, bubble, kitten Row 3: dress, hill, parrot, raccoon

Activity Worksheet: Page 33 The students are to circle the word that tells the location of the double consonants by circling either the word 'middle' or the word 'end.' On the line provided the double consonants heard are printed. **Answer Key:** Row 1: end, ss; middle, dd; middle, pp; end, ll; **Row 2:** end, ss; middle, tt; middle, bb; middle, tt **Row 3:** end, ss; end, ll; middle, rr; middle, cc

Day 3: On a chart record the following exercise consisting of sounds and words. Sounds: g, nn, ll, m, l, bb, tt, y, b, z, v **Words:** 1. pe___y 2. wa___on 3. bu___y 4. je___y 5. le___on 6. pi___ot 7. go___le 8. mi___en 9. ri___er 10. co___y The students are to supply the single or double consonants to complete each word. **Answer Key:** 1. nn 2. g 3. nn 4. ll 5. m 6. l 7. bb 8. tt 9. v 10. z

Picture Key: Row 1: mitten, money, story, hammer Row 2: baker, cabbage, zero, ladder Row 3: balloon, slippers, skull, spider Row 4: egg, doll, happy, puddle

Activity Worksheet: Page 34 The students are to print the single or double consonants heard in the middle or at the end of each picture. **Answer Key:** Row 1: tt, n, r, mm Row 2: k, bb, r, dd Row 3: ll, pp, ll, d Row 4: gg, ll, pp, dd

Day 4: The students are to listen for the double or single consonants that are heard in the middle of each word. Say the following words: 1. pepper (2 p's) 2. blossom (2 s's) 3. button (2 t's) 4. pupil (1 p) 5. cabin (1 b) 6. rotten (2 t's) 7. stable (1 b) 8. hotel (1 t) 9. swallow (2 l's) 10. broken (1 k) Have them listen for double or single consonants at the end of these words. 1. class (2 s's) 2. lemon (1 m) 3. spill (2 l's) 4. camel (1, l) 5. puff (2 f's) 6. river (1 v) 7. bed (1 d) 8. cross (2 s's) 9. bacon (1 n) 10. hog (1 g)

Activity Worksheet: Page 35 The students are to locate words that end with single or double consonants in the word search and then print them beside their meanings below. **Answer Key:** 1. gobble 2. carrot 3. bottle 4. cabbage 5. tires 6. seven 7. rabbit 8. summer 9. robin 10. city 11. lollipop 12. camel 13. gallop 14. penny

Day 5: Auditory Test on the Recognition of the position of Initial, Medial, and Final Consonant Sounds: **Instructions:** I am going to say a word and the name of a consonant. Circle the letter **B** if the consonant is at the beginning of the word; **M** if it is in the middle of the word; or **E** if it is at the end of the word. **Words:** 1. plaza (z) 2. cottage (tt) 3. hand (d) 4. frog (g) 5. bless (ss) 6. pebble (bb) 7. village (ll) 8. rabbit (bb) 9. canoe (n) 10. ladder (dd) **Answer Key:** 1. M 2. M 3. E 4. E 5. E 6. M 7. M 8. M 9. M 10. M

B. Visual Discrimination Test on the Initial, Medial and Final Consonants. Students are to record the missing consonants in the word that describes each picture. **Picture Key:** Row 1: seven, baby, kitten, squirrel Row 2: jelly, well, penny, mitten, Row 3: bell wagon, fire, hammer **Answer Key:** Words should be spelled the same way as the Picture Key.

Name: _____   Day 1 | Week 5

Often you can **hear** and **see** a **consonant** in the **middle** of a word.

Examples: baker, paper, fire

Complete the words below each picture with the missing **middle** consonant.

Use these consonants: **m n b r g t d v l**

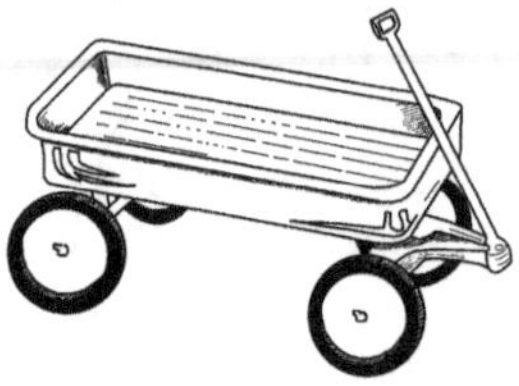 wa ___ on	 ca ___ el	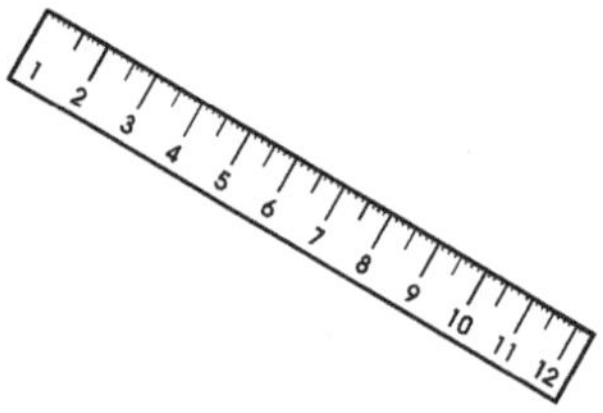 ru ___ er	 la ___ y
se ___ en	 dra ___ on	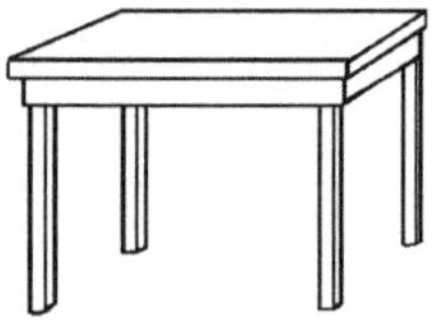 ta ___ le	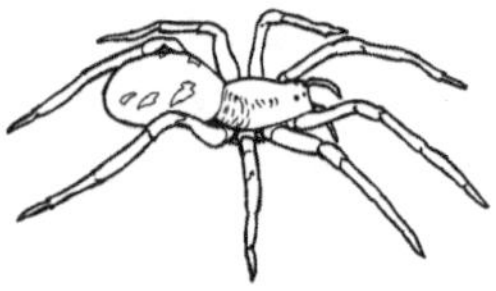 spi ___ er
 ro ___ in	 ma ___ ch	 ti ___ er	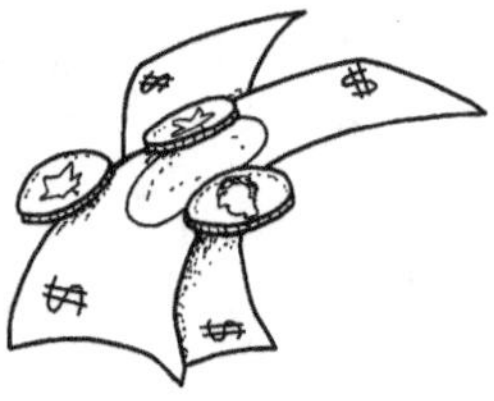 mo ___ ey
 fi ___ e	 ba ___ y	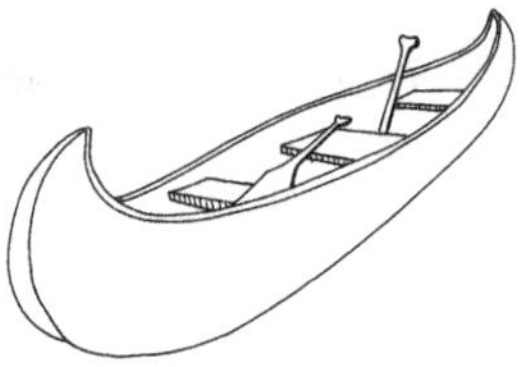 ca ___ oe	 le ___ on

Name: _____ Day 2 | Week 5

There are times when a pair of double consonants may appear in the **middle** of a word or at the **end** or it.

Examples: happy sunny furry kiss tell huff

Circle the word 'middle' or 'end' to tell where you hear the double consonant pair in each word.

Print the double consonants that you hear in the word on the line.

 middle end ___	 middle end ___	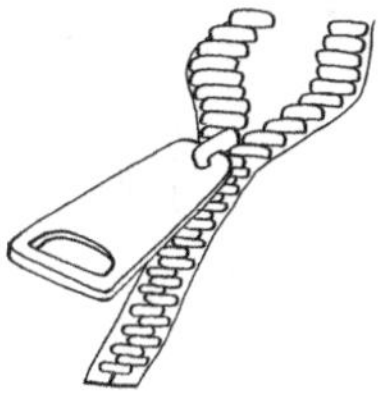 middle end ___	 middle end ___
 middle end ___	 middle end ___	 middle end ___	 middle end ___
 middle end ___	 middle end ___	 middle end ___	 middle end ___

Name: _____ Day 3 | Week 5

Many words have **single** or **double** consonants in the **middle** or at the **end** of them.

Can you tell which words have a single or double consonant?

Use these sounds to complete the words under their pictures.

dd   pp   ll   gg   d   r   bb   k   mm   n   tt

mi ___ en	mo ___ ey	sto ___ y	ha ___ er
ba ___ er	ca ___ age	ze ___ o	la ___ er
ba ___ oon	sli ___ ers	sku ___	spi ___ er
e ___ s	do ___	ha ___ y	pu ___ le

Name: _____   Day 4 | Week 5

 Can you find the words in the word search that have a single or a pair of consonants in the middle or at the end.

Circle the word and then match it to its meaning.

```
a c d f g m n o p q r s t u v w x y z a b c d e f g h i
u c a b b a g e s t r q p o n g a l l o p m i s e v e n
v w x y z a d i m i n o p q r s t u v w x y z x f j g h
i h g f c e b j k r i h g c a b o t t l e a j y c d e l
d e f g o b b l e e i e l k l d b z y x w v u p b o s r
e f g d c b a x u s s q o f e s e v e n l m n g p q r s
r o b i n h i y z v w r l p o u n m i l g f e a b a w y
a s r q p o n m l k j t l x y m z a b c h j k e c d x y
b s r c a r r o t k j b i i h m g f e d c a m e l o p q
b f a x u r o n k a z c p j k e s r q n i l m n w v u t
i e b p e n n y i b y o o x w r v u t o t l j i g d c a
t d c z w t q p m d c u p e f g h i j p y m k h f e b z
```

Meanings:
1. the way a turkey talks
2. an orange vegetable
3. It holds water.
4. a green vegetable
5. a car has four
6. a number after six
7. an animal with big ears
8. a hot time of the year
9. a spring bird
10. a large place to stay at
11. It is a kind of sucker.
12. an animal with a hump
13. the way a horse runs
14. one cent

Words:
_____
_____
_____
_____
_____
_____
_____
_____
_____
_____
_____
_____
_____
_____

Name: _____ Day 5 | Week 5

A. Auditory Test on the Recognition of the Position of Initial, Middle and Final Consonant Sounds.

1. B M E	2. B M E	3. B M E	4. B M E	5. B M E
6. B M E	7. B M E	8. B M E	9. B M E	10. B M E

B. Visual Discrimination Test on the Initial, Middle, and Final Consonat Sounds.

SSR1141 ISBN: 9781771586870 36 © On The Mark Press

Week 6: Short Vowel Sounds 'Aa' and 'Ii'

Objective: To make students aware of the short vowel sounds made by the letters 'Aa' and 'Ii.'

Day 1: Record the following story on a chart or a smart board about *'Candy Cat.'*
<u>Candy</u> <u>Cat</u> was <u>Pam's</u> pet. She was <u>black</u> with white paws. <u>Candy</u> loved to <u>dash</u> after gray mice <u>that</u> <u>ran</u> about <u>Pam's</u> house. Outside <u>Candy</u> <u>ran</u> to <u>catch</u> birds <u>standing</u> in the <u>grass</u>. In the house <u>Candy</u> liked to <u>nap</u> by the <u>back</u> door on a soft <u>mat</u>. Underline the words that contain the short a sound. Read the story to your students and then have your students read it with you. Draw their attention to the underlined words. Have them say the words. Ask: What do you notice about each underlined word. (It has the letter 'a' inside each word. It says 'ah' and the sound makes your jaw drop when you say the word.

Picture Key: Row 1: sack, rain, apple, whale Row 2: glass, flag, chair, cap Row 3: match, pail, lamp, mask

Activity Worksheet: Page 38 The students are to colour only the pictures with the short a sound. **Answer Key:** Pictures to be coloured: sack, apple, glass, flag, cap, match, lamp, mask

Day 2: Review the short 'a' sound. Have the students listen to each of the following words. If the word has the short 'a' sound they are to raise their hands. **Words:** 1. hand 2. paper 3. bath 4. cave 5. camp 6. plant 7. stairs 8. cape 9. cap 10. stamp On a chart, print the following words and have the students say them. **Words:** 1. bad 2. bag 3. map 4. wax 5. hat 6. jam 7. sat 8. gas 9. pat 10. dad

Picture Key: Row 1: hat, sad, can, tap Row 2: man, bat, jam, ant

Activity Worksheet: Page 39 The students are to spell the word to match each picture and use them to complete the following sentences. **Answer Key:** <u>Pictures</u> - Row 1: hat, sad, can, tap Row 2: man, bat, jam, ant <u>Sentences</u> - 1. ant 2. tap 3. can 4. sad 5. jam 6. man 7. bat 8. hat

Day 3: Print the words big, fit, hill on a chart. Have the students read the words. Discuss with them how the words are similar. They all have the letter 'i.' The letter 'i' often makes the 'ih' sound. Have them listen to the following story for words that have the short vowel sound.
Story: In a <u>big</u> castle surrounded by a <u>thick</u> stone wall <u>lived</u> a young <u>prince</u> called <u>Iggy</u> and <u>his</u> <u>sister</u> <u>Princess</u> <u>Isabella</u>. <u>Prince</u> <u>Iggy</u> loved to play <u>tricks</u> on <u>his</u> <u>sister</u>. One day he <u>hid</u> all of her toys <u>in</u> the castle <u>attic</u>. He also put a <u>goldfish</u> <u>in</u> her soup, a baby <u>chick</u> <u>in</u> her closet and a <u>cricket</u> in her bed. <u>Isabella</u> became tired of <u>his</u> <u>tricks</u> and told their father, the <u>King</u>, about <u>Iggy's</u> <u>tricks</u>. The <u>King</u> decided to play a <u>trick</u> on <u>Iggy</u> to teach <u>him</u> a lesson. The <u>King</u> told <u>Iggy</u> that he had <u>hidden</u> a special <u>gift</u> for <u>him</u> <u>in</u> the castle and he had to look for <u>it</u>. <u>Iggy</u> looked all over the castle for days. When he finally found the <u>gift</u>, he opened the box and there was nothing inside. <u>Iggy</u> gave up playing <u>tricks</u> on <u>his</u> <u>sister</u>. Have the students recall words from the story that have a short 'i' sound and record them on the chart. Read the words with the students and have them notice that the short vowel 'i' is found mainly inside words.

Picture Key: Row 1: dish, bed, kick, can Row 2: pig, mask, swing, tent Row 3: whiskers, fish, nose, ring Row 4: mitt, cup, bridge, cap

Activity Worksheet: Page 40 The students are to circle and colour the pictures that have the short 'i' vowel sound. Answer Key: Row 1: dish, kick Row 2: pig, swing 3. whiskers, fish, ring Row 4: mitt, bridge

Day 4: Use the following clues to review the short vowel sounds of 'a' and 'i.' Divide a chart into two columns. Print the vowels 'a' and 'e' at the top of the columns. Say a word and have the students tell which column the word should be recorded in. **Words:** 1. slam 2. smell 3. smash 4. apple 5. bread 6. band 7. chest 8. peck 9. ramp 10. spell 11. flap 12. help

Picture Key: Row 1: lid, pig, pin, bib Row 2: lip, wig, tin, sit

Activity Worksheet: Page 41 The students are to spell the word to match each picture and then use them to complete the sentences. **Answer Key:** <u>Pictures:</u> Row 1: lid, pig, pin, bib Row 2: lip, wig, tin, sit <u>Sentence Answers:</u> 1. sit 2. bib 3. tin 4. pin 5. lid 6. lip 7. wig 8. pig

Day 5: A: Auditory Test on the Recognition of the Short 'a' and 'i'
Instructions: I am going to say a word and you are to circle the vowel sound that you hear in it. **Words:** 1. swing 2. dance 3. smack 4. pinch 5. clash 6. wing 7. twig 8. raft 9. snip 10. wink **Answer Key:** 1. short i 2. short a 3. short a 4. short i 5. short a 6. short i 7. short i 8. short a 9. short i 10. short i

B. Visual Discrimination Test on the Short Vowels 'a' and 'i'
Students are to record the missing vowel sound in each word to match each picture. **Picture Key**: Row 1: candle, swing, stamp Row 2: skip, mask, grin Row 3: candy, whip, bank Row 4: bat, swim, dig
Answer Key: Row 1: a, i, a   Row 2: i, a, i   Row 3: a, i, a   Row 4: a, i, i

Name: _____ Day 1 | Week 6

In many words you will find the letter 'Aa.'

The letter 'Aa' can make two sounds.

It has a **long** sound when it says its own name and a **short** sound that says '**ah**' like in Candy Cat

Colour only the pictures that have the short '**a**' sound as in Candy Cat.

Name: _____ Day 2 | Week 6

Now that you know the sound that the short vowel 'a' says, **spell** the word that matches each picture.

Use the words that you printed in the sentences.

_____	_____	_____	_____

_____	_____	_____	_____

1. The little black _____ ran into the hole to hide from the birds.

2. Turn on the _____ to get some hot water to wash your hands.

3. Open the big _____ of soup for us to eat for supper.

4. I feel _____ when I have no one to play with.

5. I like to put _____ on my toast for breakfast.

6. My dad is a tall _____ with black hair and blue eyes.

7. A _____ likes to fly at night to catch bugs for it to eat.

8. The wind blew my _____ off my head and it landed in a puddle.

Name: _____   Day 3 | Week 6

The **short vowel 'i'** is often found in many words.

Examples: sit, fix, lip, tick

Circle and **colour** all of the pictures in the boxes that have the **short vowel 'i'** vowel sound

  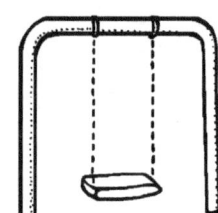 

  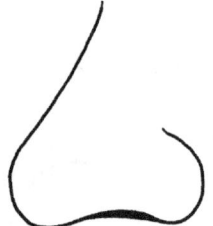 

Name: _____   Day 4 | Week 6

Now that you know the sound that the **short vowel 'i'** says, spell the word that matches each picture.

_____	_____	_____	_____
			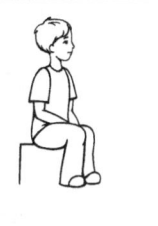
_____	_____	_____	_____

Use the words that you printed under the pictures in the sentences.

1. Please _____ in the chair by the door.

2. The baby boy had food all over his _____.

3. Open a _____ of chicken soup for your lunch.

4. We played the game called _____ the Tail on the Donkey at the party.

5. Put the _____ on the pot and let the water get hot.

6. The boy cut his _____ when he fell down the hill.

7. The girl wore a brown _____ in the play.

8. The mother _____ had to feed nine babies.

Name: _____ Day 5 | Week 6

A. Auditory Test on the Recognition of Short Vowels 'a' and 'i'

1. a i	2. a i	3. a i	4. a i	5. a i
6. a i	7. a i	8. a i	9. a i	10. a i

B. Visual Discrimination Test on the Short Vowels 'a' and 'i'

c ___ ndle	sw ___ ng	st ___ mp
sk ___ p	m ___ sk	gr ___ n
c ___ ndy	wh ___ p	b ___ nk
b ___ t	sw ___ m	d ___ g

Week 7: Recognition of the Short Vowel 'Uu'

Objective: To introduce the short vowel 'u' and review the short vowels 'a' and 'i'

Day 1: Introduce the short 'u' sound with the following story called '**Ulric the Walrus**.'
Story: Ulric was a plump walrus with two long, white tusks. Ulric lived in a land filled with much ice and snow. He liked to lie on the ice like a big lump of mud while he hunted for food. When he saw some plump fish swim by Ulric would jump up and dive into the cold water to catch some and bring them back to shore. Ulric enjoyed munching on them for his lunch on the icy shore. On a chart record the word Ulric at the top. Discuss the sound that his name begins with. Explain that the letter '**Uu**' has two sounds. It has a long sound when it says its own name and a short sound that says 'uh.' Reread the story and have your students pick out the words that have the short 'u' sound and record them on the chart under his name.

Picture Key: Row 1: brush, bat, cub, drum Row 2: pig, stamp, thumb, sack Row 3: duck, lamp, pump, mat

Activity Worksheet: Page 44 The students are to colour only the short 'u' words. **Answer Key:** Pictures to be coloured are: Row 1: brush, cub, drum Row 2: thumb Row 3: duck, pump,

Day 2: Review the short 'a, i, and u' vowel sounds. Say one of the following words and have students tell which short sound is heard in it. **Words:** junk (u) 2. tramp (a) 3. wind (i) 4. yank (a) 5. trunk (u) 6. trick (i) 7. branch (a) 8. sting (i) 9. chance (a) 10. hump (u)

Picture Key: Row 1: nut, bug, tub, bus Row 2: gun, sun, cup, jug

Activity Worksheet: Page 45 The students are to spell the words to match each picture and use them to complete the sentences. **Answer Key:** Pictures: Row 1: nut, bug, tub, bus Row 2: gun, sun, cup, jug Sentences: 1. jug 2. bug 3. bus 4. nut 5. gun 6. sun 7. cup 8. tub

Day 3: Review the short vowel sounds heard in 'u, i, and a' with the following riddles. Print the answers on a chart. **Riddles:** I am a kind of bird that quacks. (duck) 2. It is a large boat that travels on the ocean. (ship) 3. People do this together when music is played. (dance) 4. It is a smelly animal with black and white fur. (skunk) 5. It takes cars and trucks over deep water. (bridge) 6. I am found on a beach. (sand) 7. You can do this with a piece of rope. (skip) 8. It flies on a tall pole outside buildings. (flag) 9. It is small and is used to play hockey. (puck) 10. A top can do this for a long time. (spin) Have the students circle the vowel sound heard in each word on the chart.

Picture Key: Row 1: pin, bat, gum, six Row 2: jam, cub, mud, jug

Activity Worksheet: Page 46 The students will print the word for each picture and then use the words to complete the sentences. Answer Key: Pictures: Row 1: pin, bat, gum, six Row 2: jam, cub, mud, jug Sentences: 1. bat 2. gum 3. cub 4. jam 5. mud 6. six 7. jug 8. pin

Day 4: Review the short vowels 'a, i and u.' Record the following words with missing vowel sounds on a chart. **Words:** d __ g, d __ g; b __ g, b __ g, b __ g; t __ n, t __ n; p __ ck, p __ ck, p __ ck; b __ t, b __ t, b __ t; c __ p, c __ p; f __ n, f __ n, f __ n; h __ t, h __ t, h __ t **Words to be Made:** dig, dug; bag, big, bug; tan, tin; pack, pick, puck; bat, bit, but; cap, cup; fan, fin, fun; hat, hit, hut

Activity Worksheet: Page 47 The students are to choose the correct word and print it on the line in the sentence. **Answer Key:** 1. duck 2. wish 3. sock 4. wag 5. set 6. stuck 7. camp 8. wing 9. sack 10. limp

Day 5: Auditory Test on the Recognition of the Short Vowel Sounds 'a, i, and u.'
Instructions: I am going to say a word and you are to circle the vowel sound that you hear in it.
Words: 1. tub 2. kick 3. back 4. dust 5. stick 6. tank 7. zip 8. thud 9. blind 10. trap
Answer Key: 1. u 2. i 3. a 4. u 5. i 6. a 7. i 8. u 9. i 10. a

B. Visual Discrimination Test on the Short Vowels 'a, i, u': Students are to record the missing vowel sound in each word to match each picture. **Picture Key:** 1. pump 2. swing 3. match 4. gift 5. skunk 6. candy 7. fish 8. drum 9. stamp 10. stump 11. grass 12. trunk 13. bunch 14. tag 15. chick 16. brush
Answer Key: 1. short u 2. short i 3. short a 4. short i 5. short u 6. short a 7. short i 8. short u 9. short a 10. short u 11. short a 12. short u 13. short u 14. short a 15. short i 16. short u

Name: _____ Day 1 | Week 7

In many words the letter 'Uu' is often found. The letter 'Uu' can make **two** sounds.

It has a long sound when it says its own name and a short sound that says 'uh' like in 'Ulric Walrus.'

Colour only the pictures that have the **short** 'u' sound.

  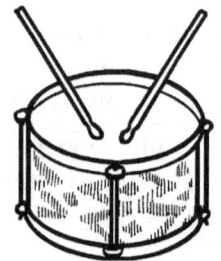

   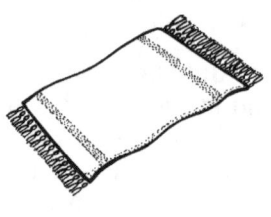

Name: _____   Day 2 | Week 7

Now that you know the sound that the **short 'u'** makes, spell the word that matches each picture on the line in each box.

		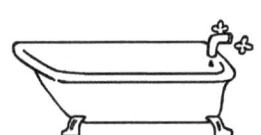	
_____	_____	_____	_____

_____	_____	_____	_____

Use the words that you made to finish the sentences below.

1. Please fill the _____ with cold milk.

2. The big, black _____ slowly walked on the window of my bedroom.

3. Some boys and girls ride to school on a big, yellow _____.

4. The squirrel picked up the _____ and ran up the side of a tree.

5. A _____ can hurt many people and animals.

6. The _____ makes boys and girls want to play outside.

7. The girl filled her _____ with cold water.

8. I had a bath in a big, white _____ that had little feet.

Name: _____   Day 3 | Week 7

You now know three short vowel sounds. They are the short **a**, short **i**, and the short **u**.

Spell the word that matches each picture on the line in each box.

		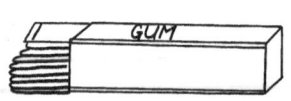	6
_____	_____	_____	_____

_____	_____	_____	_____

Use the words that you made and print them in the sentences.

1. The boy hit the ball far with the _____.

2. You should not chew _____ in the classroom at your school.

3. The _____ was lost and could not find his mother.

4. I like to put _____ on my toast.

5. Pigs like to roll in _____ in their pens on the farm.

6. I have _____ kinds of toy cars to play with and have fun.

7. You will find milk in the big yellow _____.

8. The little girl had a pretty _____ on her dress.

Name: _____ Day 4 | Week 7

 You know the sounds that the short vowels '**a, i,** and **u**' make.
Now you can use the sounds to discover **new** words.
Complete each sentence with the correct word.

1. The _____ liked to swim across the pond to visit its friends.
   (buck, duck, luck)

2. The girl made a _____ then blew out the candles on her cake.
   (fish, dish, wish)

3. The boy lost his _____ and then found it under his bed.
   (sick, sack, sock)

4. A dog likes to _____ its tail when it is happy.
   (wag, bag, sag)

5. Please _____ the table with the blue dishes.
   (sit, sat, set)

6. The car was _____ in the deep snow on the road.
   (stick, stack, stuck)

7. This summer I am going to a _____ for two weeks.
   (damp, lamp, camp)

8. The little bird hurt its _____ and could not fly.
   (sing, king, wing)

9. The man put all the potatoes in a big brown _____.
   (sick, sock, sack)

10. The dog hurt its leg and had to _____ to get around.
    (lamp, lump, limp)

Name: _____   Day 5 | Week 7

A. Auditory Test on the Short Vowels 'a, i, and u'

1. a i u	2. a i u	3. a i u	4. a i u	5. a i u
6. a i u	7. a i u	8. a i u	9. a i u	10. a i u

B. Visual Discrimination Test on the Short Vowels 'a, i, and u'

p __ mp	sw __ ng	m __ tch	g __ ft
sk __ nk	c __ ndy	f __ sh	dr __ m
st __ mp	st __ mp	gr __ ss	tr __ nk
b __ nch	t __ g	ch __ ck	br __ sh

Week 8: Introduction of the Short Vowel 'Oo' ; Review of Short Vowels 'Aa, Ee, Ii, Uu'

Objective: To make students aware of the sound made by the short vowel 'Oo'

Day 1: Introduce the short vowel 'o' using this story called 'The Otter Pups.' Olive and Ollie are otter pups. They live in a den called a holt on the rocky bank of a long river. Olive and Ollie love to frolic and flop in the river at a favourite spot. They often travel down a long waterslide that they made at the edge of the river. Olive and Ollie like to toss around and bat about small rocks while playing or use them to break open shellfish. The Otter Pups also eat fish and frogs. Record the word 'otter' on a chart and discuss the initial sound. What sound do you see at the beginning of 'otter?' (o) What does the letter 'o' say? (aw) Explain that this is the sound made by the short vowel 'o' in words. Have the students listen to each sentence of the story again for words that contain the short vowel 'o' and then record them on the chart.

Picture Key: Row 1: block, pen, sock, apple, fish Row 2: crab, fox, duck, mop, top Row 3: box, candle, rock, elf, dog Row 4: pig, frog, log, skunk, gift

Activity Worksheet: Page 50 The students are to underline and colour only the pictures with the short vowel 'o.' **Answer Key:** Row 1: block, sock Row 2: fox, mop, top Row 3: box, rock, dog Row 4: frog, log

Day 2: Review all the short vowel sounds using this listening activity. The students are to listen to each word that you say and then tell the vowel sound heard in each one. **Words:** 1. cloth (ŏ) 2. prance (ă) 3. melt (ĕ) 4. dock (ŏ) 5. fluffy (ŭ) 6. pinch (ĭ) 7. bench (ĕ) 8. thump (ŭ) 9. foggy (ŏ) 10. dull (ŭ) 11. song (ŏ) 12. hunk (ŭ)

Picture Key: Row 1: pot, mop, log, top Row 2: dog, box, fox, hop

Activity Worksheet: Page 51 The students are to spell the word for each picture and print it on the line. The words are then to be used to complete the sentences. **Answer Key:** Pictures: pot, mop, log, top Row 2: dog, box, fox, hop Sentences: 1. hop 2. top 3. log 4. mop 5. pot 6. fox 7. box 8. dog

Day 3: Review the five short vowels with this activity. On a chart print the following words leaving room for circling. **Words:** pit; win; smell; flap; bong; ham; thud; rob Have the students look at and read the words on the chart. Then have them circle the word that means: 1. a deep hole (pit) 2. to steal things or money (rob) 3. a kind of meat (ham) 4. a loud sound (thud) 5. to beat someone in a game (win) 6. to breathe with your nose (smell) 7. birds do this with their wings (flap) 8. a loud sound made by a big clock (bong)

Picture Key: Row 1: sock, pump, raft, nest Row 2: tent, grin, log, mug

Activity Worksheet: Page 52 The students are to spell the word for each picture and then use the words to complete the sentences. **Answer Key:** Pictures - Row 1: sock, pump, raft, nest Row 2: tent, grin, log, mug Sentences: 1. pump 2. raft 3. sock 4. mug 5. log 6. nest 7. grin 8. tent

Day 4: Review the short vowels 'a, e, i, o and u' using this activity. Record the five vowels down one side of a chart. The students are to listen to the words that you say and classify them to the vowel sounds heard inside each one on the chart. **Words:** 1. puck (ŭ) 2. lock (ŏ) 3. trash (ă) 4. spell (ĕ) 5. prince (ĭ) 6. thump (ŭ) 7. flop (ŏ) 8. stand (ă) 9. bench (ĕ) 10. jingle (ĭ)

Activity Worksheet: Page 53 The students are to record the missing word in each sentence using the words in the Word Box. **Answer Key:** 1. black, trot 2. Bugs trash 3. pick, pear 4. dug, mud 5. read, big 6. hut, shut 7. wind, off 8. cross, busy 9. big, bunch 10. bear, den 11. fun, rink 12. lamp, bed

Day 5: Auditory Test on the Recognition of the Short Vowel Sounds 'a, e, i, o, and u' Page 54
Instructions: I am going to say a word and you are to circle the vowel sound that you hear in it.
Words: 1. pant 2. wrist 3. cloth 4. buzzer 5. feather 6. print 7. wrong 8. trust 9. press
Answer Key: 1. a 2. i 3. o 4. u 5. e 6. i 7. o 8. u 9. e

Visual Discrimination Test on the Short Vowels 'a, e, i, o, u': Students are to record the missing vowel sound in each word to match each picture. **Picture Key:** Row 1: trash, milk, clock, rug Row 2: shell, grass, gift, frog Row 3: trunk, belt, crab, king **Answer Key:** Row 1: a, i, o, u Row 2: e, a, i, o Row 3: u, e, a, i

Name: _____ Day 1 | Week 8

The short vowel 'o' is also found in many words.
Examples: cot, log, fox, drop
Underline and **colour** all of the pictures in the boxes that have the **short vowel 'o'** sound.

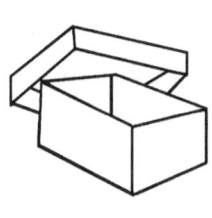    

Name: _____ Day 2 | Week 8

Now that you know the sound that the **short 'o'** says, **spell** the word that matches each picture on the line in each box.

Use the words that you made and print them in the sentences.

1. The rabbit was hurt and it could only _____ on three legs.

2. The boy made the _____ spin very fast on the floor.

3. Under the _____ lived a black and white animal that was smelly.

4. Please use the dust _____ to clean the floor in your bedroom.

5. On the stove sat a _____ full of very hot water.

6. The _____ hid behind the barn so the chickens could not see him.

7. Please put all of your toys in the toy _____ now!

8. The _____ happily wagged its tail when he found a bone.

Name: _____ Day 3 | Week 8

 The **sounds** that the **vowels** make help us to know what words say and help us to spell them.

The short vowel sounds '**a, e, i, o,** and **u**' are used in many words.

Use these sounds to spell the word for each picture. Then complete each sentence with the correct word.

 _____	 _____	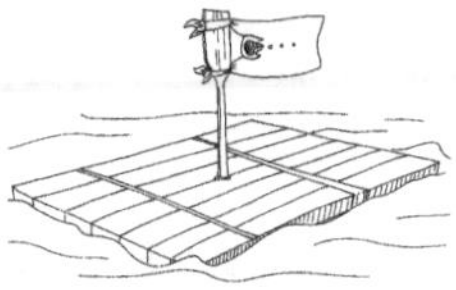 _____	 _____
 _____	 _____	 _____	 _____

1. A _____ is able to bring cold water from a well to drink.

2. The two boys sailed quickly on the river with their _____.

3. The boy could only find one _____ in his chest.

4. My _____ is full of hot chocolate to drink.

5. The old _____ was a home for two little chipmunks.

6. The robin laid three blue eggs in her _____ in the maple tree.

7. The little boy had a happy _____ on his face when he won the race.

8. The _____ was set up in a big park near a river.

Name: _____   Day 4 | Week 8

 Knowing the **short vowel sounds** helps you to read and spell words easily.

Use the words found in the **Word Box** to complete each of the following sentences.

Word Box

| bugs | pear | read | shut | black | trash | big | trot | mud | wind | pick | busy |
| hut | dug | cross | bear | fun | lamp | den | rink | bed | big | off | bunch |

1. I watched the big _____ horse _____ across the road.

2. _____ like to crawl in _____ bins for something to eat.

3. I will _____ the big yellow _____ from the tree to eat.

4. The little pup _____ a hole in the wet _____.

5. I _____ a good book while I sat in the _____ chair.

6. We sat in the _____ with the door _____ to keep warm.

7. The _____ blew all the leaves _____ the trees.

8. Look both ways before you _____ a _____ street.

9. The monkey ate a _____ _____ of bananas.

10. The _____ was asleep in its _____ in the big cave.

11. We had _____ at the _____ playing hockey.

12. Turn off the _____ before you go to _____.

Name: _____ Day 5 | Week 8

A. Auditory Test on the Short Vowels 'a, e, i, o, u'

1. a e i o u	2. a e i o u	3. a e i o u
4. a e i o u	5. a e i o u	6. a e i o u
7. a e i o u	8. a e i o u	9. a e i o u

B. Visual Discrimination Test on the Short Vowels 'a, e, i, o, u'

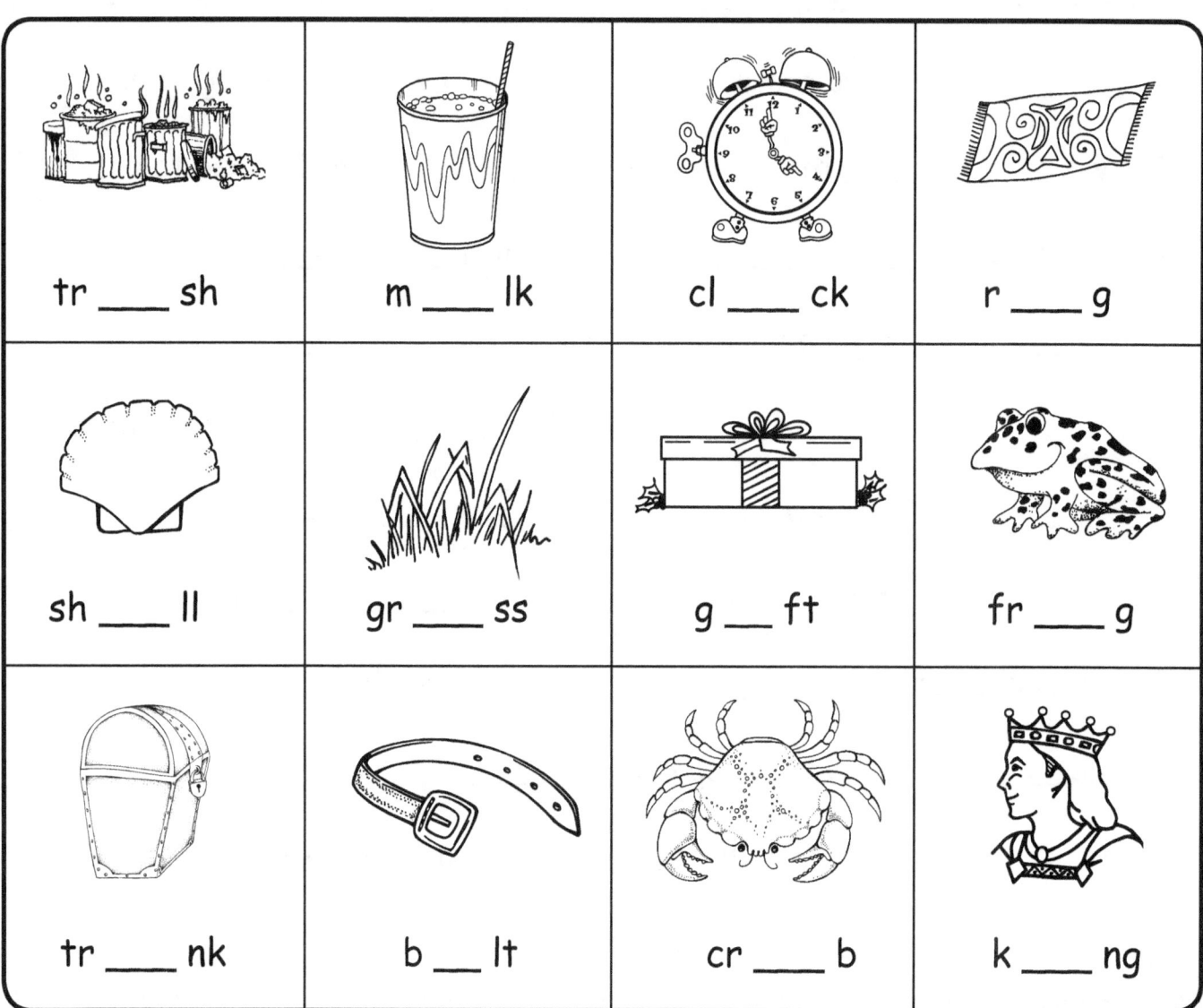

tr ___ sh   m ___ lk   cl ___ ck   r ___ g

sh ___ ll   gr ___ ss   g ___ ft   fr ___ g

tr ___ nk   b ___ lt   cr ___ b   k ___ ng

Week 9: Review of the Short Vowels 'a, e, i, o, u'

Objective: To reinforce and strengthen students' word attack skills, spelling, and comprehension skills.

Day 1: On a chart record the following groups of words. **Group 1:** bad, bed, bud, bid **Group 2:** bull, bill, ball, bell **Group 3:** bag, beg, big, bog, bug **Group 4:** sock, sack, sick, suck The teacher will say a word on the chart. The students will locate the word group and the word.

Activity Worksheet: Page 56 The students will change the vowel sound in the word at the end of the sentence to make a new word that will complete it. **Answer Key:** 1. bed 2. lift 3. sip 4. pen 5. tug 6. hot 7. hit 8. red 9. sat 10. jet 11. sack 12. tap

Day 2: On a chart record the following words: 1. mot 2. pin 3. rud 4. bus 5. fost 6. tent 7. mun 8. vost 9. lick 10. foll Have your students use the short vowel sounds to read the words silently. Then have them pick out the groups of letters that are not words. (mot, rud, fost, mun, vost) Have the students suggest a different vowel that could be used to make each incorrect group of letters become an actual word. Examples: 1. mat, met 3. red, rid, rod 5. fist, fast 7. man, men 8. vast, vest 10. fall, fill, full, fell

Picture Key: Row 1: net, bag, desk, hug, six Row 2: mask, fish, hand, log, leg

Activity Worksheet: Page 57 The students are to spell the word that matches each picture and then use each one to complete a sentence. **Answer Key:** See Picture Key for words. **Sentences:** 1. fish 2. leg 3. bag 4. mask 5. desk 6. six 7. hand 8. log 9. hug 10. net

Day 3: On a chart print the following words without vowels. Have a student record and say the name of the missing vowel and the word that it makes. **Words:** 1. h _ p 2. d _ ck 3. m _ lk 4. p _ n 5. st _ mp 6. l _ mp 7. p _ ck 8. cl _ ss 9. b _ n 9. h _ m Answers will vary.

Activity Worksheet: Page 58 The students will complete each riddle with the correct answer. **Answer Key:** 1. whiskers 2. skunk 3. trash 4. swing 5. top 6. neck 7. chest 8. pump 9. bench 10. vest

Day 4: Record the following words on a chart: stand, mend, dock, tick, plum, tracks, shop, head, grin, nut. Read each of the following clues and have the students locate the answer on the chart. Clues: 1. It is a sound that a clock makes. (tick) 2. It has a shell around it. (nut) 3. It shows a very happy feeling. (grin) 4. It means to fix something. (mend) 5. It is a round purple fruit. (plum) 6. It is an important part of your body. (head) 7. It is another word for store. (shop) 8. It is a place to park a boat. (dock) 9. A train travels on them. (tracks) 10. You do this when you sing O Canada. (stand)

Activity Worksheet: Page 59 Students are to read each sentence and answer Yes or No on the line. **Answer Key:** 1. No 2. No 3. Yes 4. No 5. No 6. Yes 7. No 8. Yes 9. No 10. No 11. Yes 12. Yes

Day 5: A. Auditory Test on the Recognition of the Short Vowel Sounds 'a,e,i,o and u.' Page 60
Instructions: I am going to say a word and you are to record on the line the short vowel sound that you hear.
Words: 1. drip 2. crush 3. chance 4. flop 5. bread 6. trick 7. hunt 8. flash 9. song 10. vent
Answer Key: 1. short i 2. short u 3. short a 4. short o 5. short e 6. short i 7. short u 8. short a 9. short o 10. short e

B. Visual Discrimination Test on the Short Vowels a, e, i, o, u. Students are to record words from the Word Box to complete each sentence.
Answer Key: 1. clock, tock 2. hid, shell 3. flag, red 4. drink, drop, pop 5. lend, best 6. flock, pond 7. dump, sand 8. camel, humps, back

Name: _____   Day 1 | Week 9

Now you know all the short vowel sounds made by the letters 'a, e, i, o, u.'

Read each sentence carefully. Change the **vowel** in the word at the **end** of each sentence to make a **new** word that fits it. **Print** the word on the line.

1. Bill fell asleep on the big _____. (bad)

2. The man had to help us _____ the big rock. (left)

3. The boy will _____ his drink with a straw. (sap)

4. Bob left his _____ on the top of his desk. (pan)

5. The little pup likes to _____ on the rope when he plays. (tag)

6. The sun was too _____ to play outside. (hit)

7. A big wind _____ the tent and made it fall down. (hat)

8. Bill has a _____ truck full of rocks. (rid)

9. The little red hen _____ on her eggs in the nest of hay. (set)

10. The big _____ landed safely on the long runway. (jot)

11. Put all the potatoes in the big brown _____. (sick)

12. Did you hear someone _____ on our back door? (tip)

Name: _____ Day 2 | Week 9

Knowing all of the short vowel sounds **helps** to make **reading** and **spelling** easier.

Spell the word for each picture on the line under it. Use each **word** that you made to **finish** each sentence.

_____ _____ _____ _____ _____

_____ _____ _____ _____ _____

1. The little _____ like to swim in the big dish.

2. The boy fell and cut his _____.

3. The big _____ was full of new toys for boys and girls.

4. The girl had a funny _____ on her face.

5. Put all of your things in your _____ before you leave.

6. There were _____ pups sleeping in the big box.

7. I print all my work with my left _____.

8. Under the _____ sat a little brown toad.

9. I like to _____ my mom when I see her.

10. My dad took my fish out of the water with a _____.

Name: _____ Day 3 | Week 9

How good are you at reading and answering riddles?
Read each riddle and **find** the answer in the **Word Box**.
Print the **answer** on the line.

Word Box

| whiskers | skunk | swing | top | pump |
| neck | vest | trash | bench | chest |

1. We are white hair. Santa Claus has some. We are _____.

2. I am an animal. I have a very bad smell. I am a _____.

3. People do not want me. I ride in a big truck to a dump. I am called _____.

4. I am a seat with ropes. I can take you up high. I am a _____.

5. I am a kind of toy. I can spin around many times. I am a _____.

6. I am part of your body. Your head sits on me. I am your _____.

7. People put things in me. I am a big box with a lock. I am called a _____.

8. I am at the top of a well. Water comes out of me. I am a _____.

9. I am a kind of seat. Many people can sit on me. I am long. I am a _____.

10. I am a kind of jacket. I do not have sleeves. I am a _____.

Name: _____ Day 4 | Week 9

Have **fun** reading and answering these silly questions!

Print the word '**yes**' on the line if the question could happen.

Print the word '**no**' if the question could not happen.

1. Can a pig go as fast as a cab? _____

2. Can a doll and a teddy bear run and catch a bus? _____

3. Can a hole in a sock be fixed? _____

4. Does a fox have brown spots all over its back? _____

5. Is a baby rabbit called a cub? _____

6. Can a mouse trap catch mice? _____

7. Does a skunk have a nice, sweet smell? _____

8. Can you start a fire with a match? _____

9. Cats and dogs like to ride on a school bus every day. _____

10. Does a frog make a nest in a tree in the spring? _____

11. It is fun to play in the sand at a beach? _____

12. Can a chipmunk climb up high in a tree? _____

Name: _____   Day 5 | Week 9

A. Auditory Test on the Recognition of the Short Vowel Sounds 'a,e,i,o,u'

1. ___	2. ___	3. ___	4. ___	5. ___
6. ___	7. ___	8. ___	9. ___	10. ___

B. Visual Discrimination Test on the Short Vowel Sounds 'a,e,i,o,u'

Word Box

back	humps	dump	flock	hid	tock
camel	sand	pond	clock	shell	flag
red	drink	best	lend	pop	drop

1. The _____ went tick-_____ all day long.

2. The big turtle _____ inside his bumpy, brown _____.

3. The _____ was _____ and white flying on the pole.

4. I will _____ every _____ of my _____.

5. I will _____ you my _____ book to read.

6. The _____ of geese flew over the _____.

7. The _____ truck was full of _____.

8. A _____ may have one or two _____ on its _____.

Week 10: Introduction of the Long Vowel Sounds 'a, e, i, o, u'

Objective: To familiarize and review the long vowels a, e, i, o, and u and their sounds

Day 1: Review the long vowel sounds 'a, e, i' with the following sentences. They could be written on a chart or said orally. Read sentence one with me. 1. The big hairy ape raced about his cage to make people laugh. Which words in the sentence have the long vowel 'a' sound, (hairy, ape, raced, cage, make) Underline the words in the sentence. Why isn't the word 'about' underlined? (It has the short 'a' vowel sound.) 2. Follow the same procedure for the long vowel 'e.' Sentence 2: The team of horses had to pull the heavy wagon through a deep creek and up a very steep hill. Underlined Words: team, deep, creek, steep Why isn't the word 'heavy' underlined? (It has the short 'e' vowel sound.) 3. Sentence 3. It was a funny sight to see the giant climb down the big vine after Jack. Underlined words: sight, giant, climb, vine Why isn't the word 'big' underlined? (It has the short 'i' vowel sound.)

Picture Key: Row 1: cane, bee, rain, pie Row 2: bike, cake, dime, leaf Row 3: vine, feet, rake, whale

Activity Worksheet: Page 62 The students are to choose the word that matches each picture. **Answer Key:** Row 1: cane, bee, rain, pie Row 2: bike, cake, dime, leaf Row 3: vine, feet, rake, whale

Day 2: Review the long vowel sounds 'o' and 'u' with the following riddles. Print the answers on a chart to discuss later. **Riddles:** 1. I am a flower that grows on a bush that has thorns. (rose) 2. I am a musical instrument. I play sweet music. (flute) 3. A dog likes to make this with its paws. (hole) 4. In the winter we feel this way. (cold) 5. At school we should never break one. (rule) 6. We use this to put food into our mouths. (fork) 7. Toothpaste comes in this kind of a container. (tube) 8. It is a kind of map shaped like a ball. (globe) Print each answer on a chart. Discuss the words. How are these words the same? (They all have long vowels.) What else is the same about the words? (They all end with the vowel 'e.') Does the 'e' make any sound? (No) Did you know that when a word ends with a silent 'e' it pinches the vowel ahead to make it shout out its own name. So if you come to a word that ends with an 'e' and it has another vowel ahead of it, what should you do? Try the long vowel sound to figure out what the word says. Try these words: cube, hope, date, mine, leave.

Picture Key: Row 1: road, cube, horse, tube, Row 2: store, mule, glue, globe

Activity Worksheet: Page 63 The students will print the picture's name on the line below each one. These words are to be used to complete the sentences. **Answer Key:** Picture Words - Row 1: road, cube, horse, tube Row 2: store, mule, glue, globe **Sentence Words** - 1. mule 2. road 3. globe 4. cube 5. store 6. glue 7. horse 8. tube

Day 3: Review all the long vowels using this activity called 'Who Can Make a Word?' On a chart print the following incomplete words. 1. wh __ le 2. b __ ne 3. t __ be 4. f __ ve 5. s __ at 6. g __ me 7. r __ de 8. r __ le 9. c __ rn 10. p __ pe The students are to put in the missing long vowel and say the word.

Activity Worksheet: Page 64 The students are to complete each sentence with words from the Word Box. **Answer Key:** 1. Rake, pile 2. baby, cute 3. toad, hide 4. Clean, soap 5. hole, bone 6. teeth, white 7. ghost, float, over 8. flake, snow, nose 9. ears, knees, feet 10. tune, flute

Day 4: A. Listen to these words: made, beat, nine, nose, blue. What vowel sound do you hear in each word. (Long a, e, i, o, and u.) When you hear vowels say their own name they are making their long sound. **B.** Listen to these words: bag, beg, big, bog, bug What vowel sounds do you hear? (short vowel sounds) Listen to these words and tell the vowel sound that you hear. Is it the long or the short vowel sound? **Words:** pair (long a); crib (short i); speak (long e); junk (short u); toe (long o); crack (short a); knife (long i); chest (short e); huge (long u); lock (short o)

Picture Key: Row 1: glue, soap, brush, Row 2: spider, clock, brick Row 3: grapes, wheel, chain Row 4: hand, slide, cube

Activity Worksheet: Page 65 The students are to classify the vowel sound heard in each word as the 'long' sound or the 'short' sound. **Answer Key:** Row 1: Long u; long o; short u Row 2: long i; short o; short i Row 3: long a, long e, long a Row 4: short a: long i; long u

Day 5: Auditory Test on the Recognition of the Long and Short Vowels a, e, i, o, u. Page 66 Instructions: I am going to say a word. You are to circle the vowel if it has the long sound or put a box around it if its the short sound. Words: 1. sneeze (circle e) 2. hunt (box u) 2. price (circle i) 4. rule (box u) 5. drop (box o) 6. cave (circle a) 7. snore (circle o) 8. sting (box i) 9. mend (box e) 10. light (circle i) 11. song (box o) 12. snore (circle o)

B. Visual Discrimination Test on the Long and Short Vowels 'a, e, i, o, u': Students are to record the missing word in each sentence. Answer Key: 1. neat 2. flock 3. hid 4. stick 5. melt 6. pile 7. hill 8. huge 9. hit 10. lane

SSR1141 ISBN: 9781771586870

Name: _____ Day 1 | Week 10

Now you know that the long vowels '**a**, **e**, and **i**' say their own names in many words.

When a vowel says its own name it is called a **long vowel**.

Use the **words** in the Word Box to **name** each picture. Print its name on the line under each picture.

Word Box
whale   leaf   pie   rain   dime   rake   cane   bee   bike   cake   vine   feet

_____	_____	_____	_____

_____	_____	_____	_____
	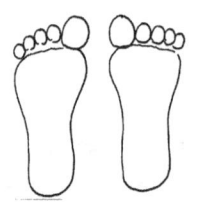		
_____	_____	_____	_____

Name: _____   Day 2 | Week 10

There are ways to remember which vowel is doing all the talking and which one is silent.

1. When two vowels go walking together in a word, the first one does the talking and shouts out its own name. It is a long vowel.

2. When a word ends with the letter 'e', it pinches the vowel ahead and makes it shout out its own name. It is a long vowel.

Match each word to its picture. Use the same words to finish the sentences.

cube   glue   globe   horse   road   store   tube   mule

1. The _____ was used to carry big loads of flour.
2. The _____ to the beach was long and bumpy.
3. A round map is called a _____.
4. I put an ice _____ in my drink to keep it cold.
5. At the _____ we got some candy and gum.
6. I used _____ to make a paper bag puppet.
7. I saw the _____ jump over the gate and run away.
8. Toothpaste comes in a _____.

Name: _____ Day 3 | Week 10

The long vowels 'a,e,i,o,u' are seen in many words.

Long vowel sounds are often heard in words that have **two** vowels walking together or in words that end with a silent 'e' that pinches the vowel ahead to shout out its own name.

Print the correct word from the Word Box on the line in each sentence.

Word Box

ears	flake	clean	rake	baby	toad	bone	soap	teeth
ghost	hole	cute	pile	snow	hide	float	nose	knees
	over	tune	feet	white	flute			

1. _____ all the leaves into one big _____.

2. The _____ girl looked _____ in her pink dress.

3. The little brown _____ hopped into the garden to _____.

4. _____ your hands with _____ and hot water.

5. The dog dug a deep _____ to hide its big _____ in.

6. The girl's _____ are clean and very _____.

7. The little _____ liked to _____ all _____ the house.

8. A _____ of _____ landed on my _____.

9. I have two _____, two _____ and two _____.

10. Can you play a _____ on your new _____.

Name: _____ Day 4 | Week 10

Which **vowel** sound do you **hear** in each word?

Is it the **long** vowel sound or the **short** vowel sound?

Print the name of the vowel sound on the line under the picture.

Examples: short vowel 'a' or long vowel 'a'

Name: _____ Day 5 | Week 10

A. Auditory Test on the Short and Long Vowels 'a,e,i,o,u'

1. a e i o u	2. a e i o u	3. a e i o u	4. a e i o u
5. a e i o u	6. a e i o u	7. a e i o u	8. a e i o u
9. a e i o u	10. a e i o u	11. a e i o u	12. a e i o u

B. Visual Discrimination Test on the Short and Long Vowels 'a,e,i,o,u'

1. Your work should always be _____. (net, neat, nest)

2. The _____ of birds were flying south. (flake, flat, flock)

3. The girls _____ behind the tree and the boys could not find them.
   (hide, head, hid)

4. I threw a _____ into the deep lake. (stuck, stack, stick)

5. When spring comes all the snow will _____. (milk, melt, mine)

6. Put all the hay into a big _____ (pile, pole, pale)

7. The children walked up the _____ to get water. (hall, hull, hill)

8. An elephant is a _____ animal. (hug, huge, hag)

9. The boy could not _____ the ball with the bat. (hat, hut, hit)

10. The girl walked down the _____ to get to her grandmother's house.
    (line, lane, lone)

Week 11 — Long and Short Vowels in Compound Words

Objective: To make students aware that compound words contain long and short vowels.

Day 1: Record the following words on a chart: airmail, airport, airplane, airline. Look at these words and tell how they are made. (Two words have been put together to make one big word.) Do you know the name given to two words put together to make one word. (They are called compound words.) Let's look at some compound words on the chart. How is each word the same. (They have long vowels in each word.) Discuss the vowel sounds made in each word: airmail - long a, long a; airport - long a, long o; airplane - long a, long a; airline - long a, long i What did you find out about compound words. (Each one is made of two words that contain vowels. The vowels may be the same or different in each word. The vowels may make long or short sounds.

Picture Key: Row 1: fireplace, raincoat, snowflake Row 2: toenail, ponytail, scarecrow Row 3: skateboard, rowboat, beehive

Activity Worksheet: Page 68 The students will complete the compound words with the missing long vowels heard in each word. **Answer Key:** Row 1: i, a; a, o; o; a Row 2: o, a; o, a; a, o Row 3: a, o; o, a; e, i

Day 2: Record the following compound words on a chart: catfish, grassland, uphill, cannot. Look at these compound words and tell how they are made. (Two words have been put together to make one big word. What are these words called? (compound words) Let's look at the words written on the chart. How is each word the same? (Each word has a short vowel sound.) Discuss the vowel sounds made in each word: catfish - short a; short i; grassland - short a, short a; uphill - short u, short i; cannot - short a, short o

Picture Key: Row 1: haystack, windmill, bathtub Row 2: nutcracker, thumbtack, eggshell Row 3: backpack, sunfish, grasshopper

Activity Worksheet: Page 69 The students are to complete each word with the correct short vowel. **Answer Key:** Row 1: a, a; i, i; a, u Row 2: u, a; u, a; e, e Row 3: a, a; u, i; a, o

Day 3: Record the following compound words on a chart: playpen, forget, inside, tiptoe. Look at these compound words and tell how they are made. (Two words with different vowel sounds have been put together to make one big word.) Discuss the vowel sounds heard in each of the following words: backbone (short a; long o) runway (short u; long a) campfire (short a; long i) tugboat (short u; long o) weekend (long e; short e)

Picture Key: Row 1: fireplace, popcorn, raincoat Row 2: bathtub, snowflake, backpack Row 3: ponytail, goldfish, pancakes Row 4: eggshell, flagpole, fireman

Activity Worksheet: Page 70 The students will complete each word with the missing vowels. **Answer Key:** Row 1: i, a; o, o; a, i Row 2: a, u; o, a; a, a Row 3: o, a; o, i; a, a Row 4: e, e; a, o; i, a

Day 4: Review long and short vowels in compound words. Record the following compound words on a chart: s__ash__ll; fl__shl__ght; cl__ssm__te; f__rg__t; s__nsh__ne; h__irc__t; j__llyf__sh; s__nsh__ne The students are to supply the missing vowels and tell if they are long or short.

Activity Worksheet: Page 71 The students are to complete each sentence using a compound word. **Answer Key:** 1. subway 2. pancakes 3. rainbow 4. buttercup, 5. tugboat 6. flashlight 7. seashells 8. scarecrow 9. rowboat 10. campfire 11. goldfish 12. firefighters

Day 5: A. Auditory Test on the Recognition of Long and Short Vowels in Compound Words: Page 72 The teacher will say a compound word and the students will circle the vowel sounds heard in each one. **Words:** 1. sandstone 2. driveway 3. sunset 4. catfish 5. stagecoach 6. runway **Answer Key:** 1. short a, long o 2. long i, long a 3. short u, short e 4. short a, short i 5. long a, long o 6. short u, long a

B. Visual Discrimination Test on the Long and Short Vowels in Compound Words:
The students will complete each compound word with long and short vowels. **Answer Key:** 1. forget 2. skateboard 3. bulldog 4. cannot 5. uphill 6. tiptoe 7. something 8. seaweed 9. snowman 10. sunshine 11. backbone 12. highchair 13. handcuffs 14. homemade 15. spaceship

Name: _____ Day 1 | Week 11

A **compound word** is a **big** word made by putting two words together.

Examples: rowboat, oatmeal, daytime

Each word has a vowel sound that can be heard. Sometimes you hear the **long vowel** in both words. The vowels may be the same or may be different.

Complete the word under each picture with the correct **long vowel** sound.

f __ repl __ ce	r __ inc __ at	sn __ wfl __ ke
t __ en __ il	p __ nyt __ il	sc __ recr __ w
sk __ teb __ ard	r __ wb __ at	b __ eh __ ve

Name: _____ | Day 2 | Week 11 |

A **compound word** is made of **two** words.

Sometimes each word has a **short vowel** sound.

Examples: bulldog, lipstick, cannot

Sometimes the vowels are the **same** or they may be **different**.

Complete the word under each picture with the correct **short vowel** sounds.

 h __ yst __ ck	 w __ ndm __ ll	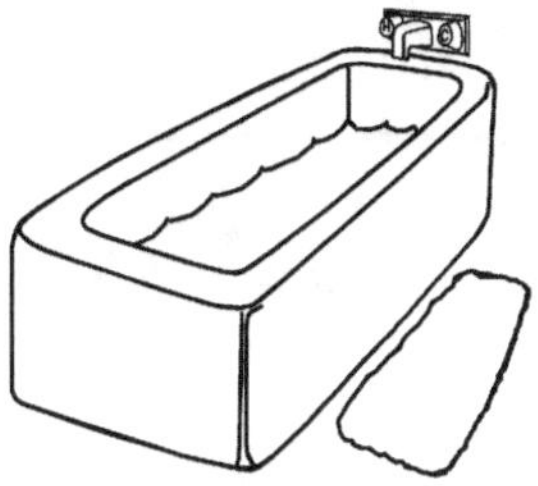 b __ tht __ b
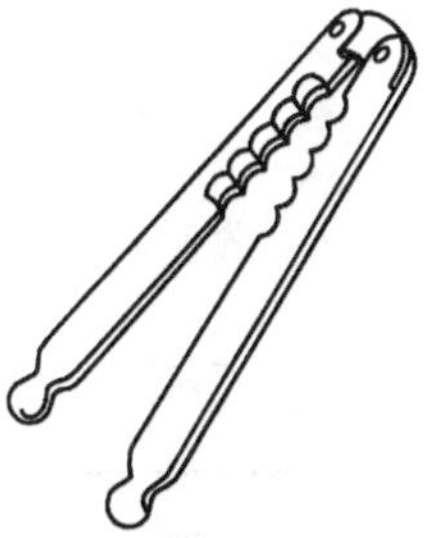 n __ tcr __ cker	 th __ mbt __ ck	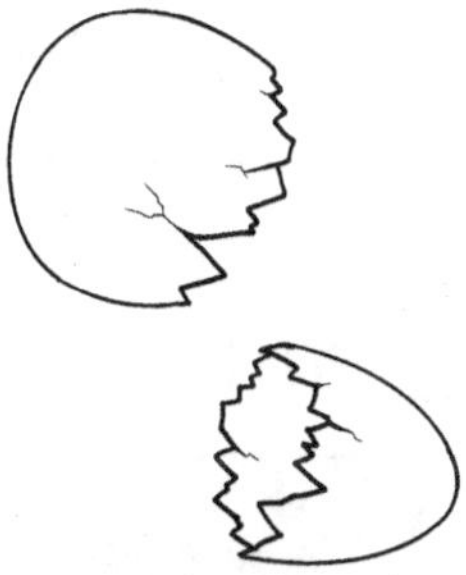 __ ggsh __ ll
 b __ ckp __ ck	 s __ nf __ sh	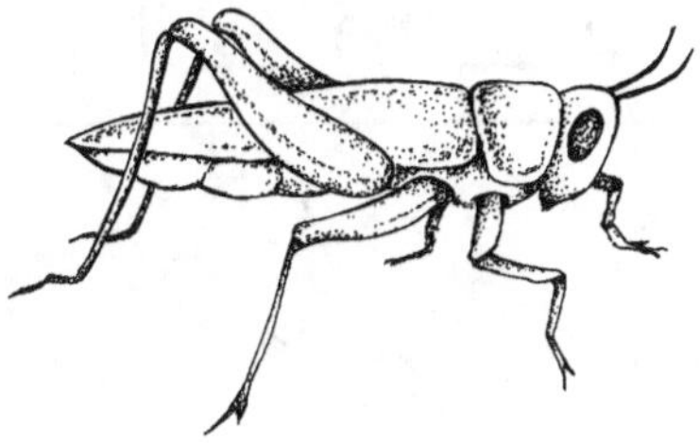 gr __ ssh __ pper

Name: _____ Day 3 | Week 11

Compound words often have **two** vowel sounds.

Sometimes you hear the **long** vowel sound in one word and the **short** vowel sound in the other word. The words may also have the **same** vowel sound.

Examples: airport   cannot   peanut   rowboat

Complete the word under each picture with the correct vowel sounds

f __ repl __ ce	p __ pc __ rn	r __ inc __ at
b __ tht __ b	sn __ wfl __ ke	b __ ckp __ ck
p __ nyt __ il	g __ ldf __ sh	p __ nc __ kes
__ ggsh __ ll	fl __ gp __ le	f __ rem __ n

Name: _____ Day 4 | Week 11

Many **compound words** have long and short vowels.

Use the compound words in the Word Box to complete each sentence.

Word Box

firefighters	subway	goldfish	campfire
pancakes	rowboat	rainbow	scarecrow
seashells	flashlight	tugboat	buttercup

1. In the city many people ride on a _____ train to get to work.

2. I love to eat _____ with maple syrup for breakfast.

3. After the storm we saw a colourful _____ in the sky.

4. A _____ is a yellow wild flower that grows in fields and along roads.

5. The _____ pulled the large ship out of the port to the ocean.

6. We used a _____ to see our way in the dark.

7. I like to pick up _____ when I go to the beach.

8. A _____ is put in a field to scare crows away from the corn.

9. I used an old _____ to take me across the river.

10. We sat around the _____ and sang songs and told stories.

11. The _____ swam around its bowl looking for food.

12. The _____ quickly put out the fire using their hoses.

Name: _____ Day 5 | Week 11

A. **Auditory Test on the Long and Short Vowel Sounds 'a,e,i,o,u' Heard in Compound Words.**

1. Long	Short	2. Long	Short
a e i o u	a e i o u	a e i o u	a e i o u
3. Long	Short	4. Long	Short
a e i o u	a e i o u	a e i o u	a e i o u
5. Long	Short	6. Long	Short
a e i o u	a e i o u	a e i o u	a e i o u

B. **Visual Discrimination Test on the Recognition of Long and Short Vowels in Compound Words**

1. f __ rg __ t	2. sk __ teb __ ard	3. b __ lld __ g
4. c __ nn __ t	5. __ ph __ ll	6. t __ pt __ e
7. s __ meth __ ng	8. s __ aw __ ed	9. sn __ wm __ n
10. s __ nsh __ ne	11. b __ ckb __ ne	12. h __ ghch __ ir
13. h __ ndc __ ffs	14. h __ mem __ de	15. sp __ cesh __ p

Week 12: Syllabication in Regular and Compound Words

Objective: To teach the rules pertaining to dividing words into syllables.

Day 1: Record the following words on a chart: hop, fat, cub, set, find. Discuss how these words are similar. (They all have one vowel and one word part called a syllable) Do they have the same vowel sound inside? (No) Which word has a different vowel sound? (find) Why is it different? (It has a long vowel while the other words have short vowels.) Record the following words on a chart: mitten, golden, chipmunk, button, elbow. Discuss how these words are similar. (They all have two word parts or syllables and two vowels. Do all the vowels make the same sound? (No, they make different sounds.) What is found in each word part? (a vowel) What have you learned today about words. (A word that has one vowel heard has one syllable. A word with two vowels heard has two syllables.)

Picture Key: Row 1: clock, monkey, spider, dime Row 2: button, mitten, vine, zebra Row 3: beehive, snowman, bike, rowboat

Activity Worksheet: Page 74 The students are to record the number of syllables heard in each word.
Answer Key: Row 1: 1, 2, 2, 1 Row 2: 2, 2, 1, 2 Row 3: 2, 2, 1, 2

Day 2: Record the following words on a chart: zipper, basket. Discuss how these words are the same. (Each one has two syllables.) Clap the word 'zipper.' Where would you divide this word into syllables, (Between the two p's.) What kind of letter is in each syllable? (a vowel) Clap the word 'basket.' Where would you divide 'basket' into syllables? (Between the two consonants in the middle of the word.) You can divide many words into syllables between two consonants. The middle consonants may be the same or they may be different. Each syllable has a vowel.

Picture Key: Row 1: kitten, monkey, rabbit, button Row 2: zipper, pillow, basket, pumpkin

Activity Worksheet: Page 75 The students are to divide each word into syllables and then use the words to complete the sentences. **Answer Key: A**: kit/ten, mon/key, rab/bit, but/ton, zip/per, pil/low, bas/ket, pump/kin **B**: 1. rabbit 2. pillow 3. basket 4. button 5. pumpkin 6. monkey 7. kitten 8. zipper

Day 3: Record the following words on a chart: table, paper, lady, crayon, maple. Have your students say the words. In what way are all the words the same. (They all have the long a sound.) Clap each word as you say it again. What do you notice about each word this time. (They all have two syllables.) Where do you think each word should be divided? (after the long vowel) Record these words on the chart: before, paper, music, maple, secret. Have the students tell where each word should be divided into syllables

Picture Key: Row 1: baker, tulip, music, tiger Row 2: spider, baby, pony, zebra

Activity Worksheet: Page 76 The students are to divide each word under the pictures into syllables with a line. Then the words are to be used to complete the following sentences. **Answer Key:** Syllables: Row 1: ba/ker, tu/lip, mu/sic, ti/ger Row 2: spi/der, ba/by, po/ny, ze/bra Sentences: 1. tiger 2. music 3. spider 4. pony 5. zebra 6. tulip 7. baker 8. baby

Day 4: Record the following words on a chart: cabin, canoe, money, city, study. Have the students read the words out loud. How many syllables do you hear in each word? (2) What kind of letter is in the middle of each word? (a consonant) Is the first vowel in each word long or short? (short) When a word has two syllables and the first syllable has a short vowel you divide the word after the consonant following the first vowel. Have the students divide the words on the chart using a slanted stroke.

Picture Key: Row 1: robin, ruler, money, seven Row 2: lemon, shovel, flower, candy

Activity Worksheet: Page 77 The students will divide the words under each picture into syllables and then use the words to complete the sentences. **Answer Key:** Row 1: ro-bin, ru/ler, mon/ey, sev/en Row 2: lem/on, shov/el, flow/er, can/dy Sentences: 1. candy 2. lemon 3. shovel 4. flower 5. seven 6. ruler 7. robin 8. money

Day 5: Syllabication Test: Auditory Test on the Number of Syllables Heard in Words Page 78
Teacher Instructions: Record the number of syllables that you hear in each word on the line in each box
Words: 1. tennis 2. pot 3. berry 4. feather 5. sneak 6. wagon 7. cabbage 8. tickle 9. stick 10. whiskers
Answer Key: 1. (2) 2. (1) 3. (2) 4. (2) 5. (1) 6. (2) 7. (2) 8. (2) 9. (1) 10. (2)

Visual Discrimination Test: Dividing Words into Syllables
The students are to record each word under the syllabication rule that it follows. **Answer Key:** Box 1: mitten, muffin, pillow, basket Box 2: baby, robot, music, pony Box 3: seven, shovel, lemon, robin

Name: _____   Day 1 | Week 12

A **syllable** is a word part that has a vowel.
Examples: top, hay, hit, tent, nut

Some words have **two** syllables. Each syllable has a vowel
Examples: butter, rainbow, pancake, goldfish

Record the **number** of **syllables** that you hear in each picture.

Syllables ___	Syllables ___	Syllables ___	Syllables ___
Syllables ___	Syllables ___	Syllables ___	Syllables ___
Syllables ___	Syllables ___	Syllables ___	Syllables ___

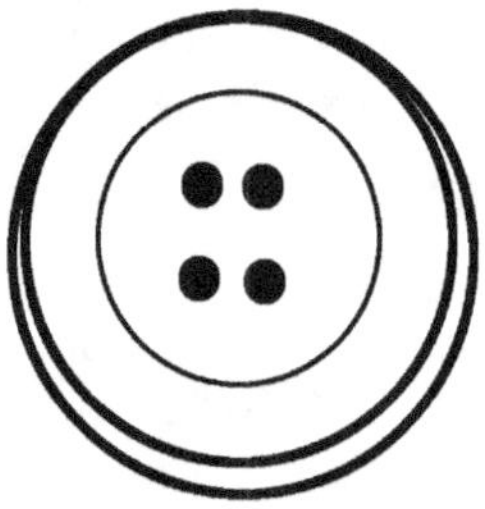

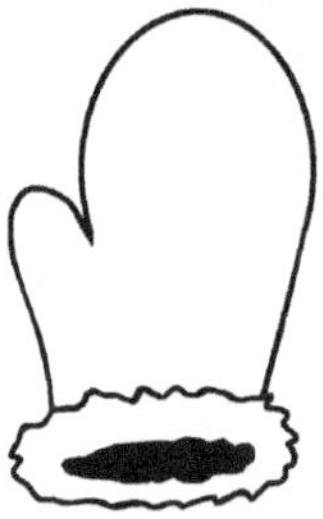

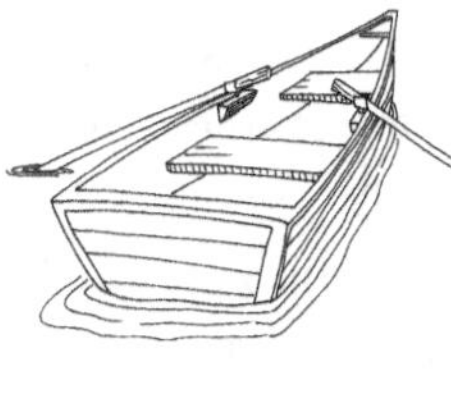

Name: _____   Day 2 | Week 12

A **syllable** is a part of a word. Each syllable has a **vowel**. Some words have only **one** syllable while others may have **two** or **more**.

Words are divided into syllables between the **two middle consonants** that are the **same** or **different**.

Examples: win/ter   sum/mer

Divide each of the following words under the pictures into syllables using a stroke /. Use the words in the sentences.

blan/ket

bas/ket

kitten	monkey	rabbit	button
zipper	pillow	basket	pumpkin

1. The _____ hopped across the road quickly.

2. I like to sleep on a soft _____ at night.

3. The little girl picked up the eggs and put them in her _____.

4. It is cold outside so _____ up your coat to keep warm.

5. Mark picked out a big _____ to make a jack-o'-lantern.

6. The _____ at the zoo did tricks to make people laugh.

7. The little _____ chased the ball of wool all over the floor.

8. A _____ is used to do up coats, pants, and boots.

Name: _____ Day 3 | Week 12

There are many words that are divided between a **consonant** and a **vowel**.

When the **first** vowel sound is **long** the word is divided **after** the vowel.

Divide each word under the pictures into **syllables** using a **stroke /**. **Circle** the vowel that you hear. Use the words to **complete** the sentences.

Examples:
ru/er   pa/per
ri/ding   bro/ken

baker   tulip   music   tiger

spider   baby   pony   zebra

1. A _____ has yellow and black stripes and can roar loudly.

2. I like to play _____ on my new flute.

3. The _____ sat and waited for a bug to fly into its web.

4. The children went for a ride on a little, white _____.

5. The little black and white _____ ran about the big cage.

6. The _____ is seen in gardens in the spring.

7. The _____ makes and bakes all kinds of bread.

8. The little _____ girl was sleeping in her crib.

Name: _____   Day 4 | Week 12

Many words are made of **two syllables**.

A word that has a **long vowel** in its first syllable is divided after the vowel.

A word that has a short vowel in its first syllable is **divided** after the **consonant**.

Divide each word under its picture into **syllables**. **Use** each word in the sentences.

Examples:
bro/ken   pic/nic

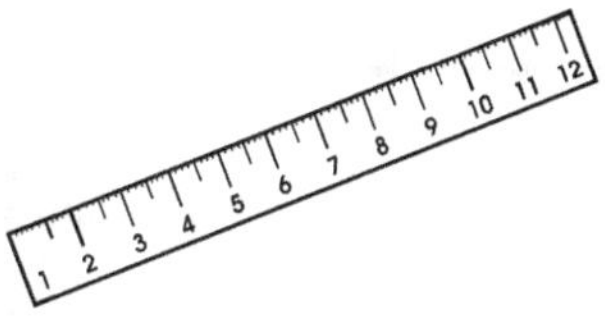

robin	ruler	money	seven
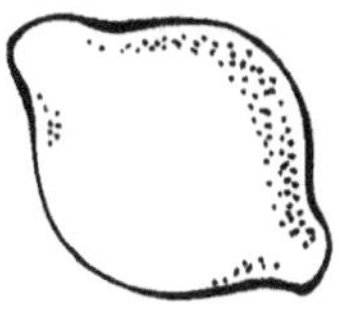 lemon	 shovel	 flower	 candy

1. Boys and girls like to get _____ on Hallowe'en night.

2. A _____ is a yellow fruit that grows on a tree.

3. I used a _____ to clear the snow from the sidewalk.

4. A pink _____ was growing in our backyard garden.

5. There are _____ Canada geese swimming on the pond.

6. You can make good lines using a _____.

7. The _____ sat and watched the worm wiggle on the grass.

8. My grandmother gave me some _____ for my birthday.

Name: _____ Day 5 | Week 12

A. Auditory Test on the Number of Syllables Heard in Each Word:

1. ___	2. ___	3. ___	4. ___	5. ___
6. ___	7. ___	8. ___	9. ___	10. ___

B. Visual Discrimination Test on Dividing Words into Syllables

Print the words in the box under the rule that it follows

shovel   seven   baby   mitten   robot   muffin
pillow   lemon   pony   music   robin   basket

fun / ny	ze / bra	can / dy
Divide between two consonants.	Divide after the first vowel if it is long.	When the first vowel is short, divide after the consonant.
___	___	___
___	___	___
___	___	___
___	___	___

Week 13: Long and Short Vowel Sounds of 'Yy'

Objective: To make students aware that the letter 'Yy' can be a vowel when it makes the long 'e' and long 'i' sound in words.

Day 1: On a chart record the following groups of words. **Group 1:** cry, dry, fry, by **Group 2:** bunny, baby, fairy, pony Have your students read aloud Group 1 words. In what way are these words the same? (They all end with the letter 'y.' What sound does the letter 'y' make? (It makes the long 'i' sound.) Have your students read the second group of words. What letter does each word end with? (the letter 'y') What sound does the letter 'y' make in this group of words? It makes the long 'e' sound. Explain to your students that the letter '**y**' can be a **vowel** or a **consonant**.

Picture Key: Row 1: canary, sky, pony Row 2: fly, bunny, cry Row 3: puppy, hockey, fry

Activity Worksheet: Page 80 The students are to record the words long 'i' or long 'e' for the sound that the letter 'y' makes in each picture. **Answer Key:** Row 1: long e, long i, long e Row 2: long i, long e, long i Row 3: long e, long e, long i

Day 2: Record the following groups of words on a chart. **Group 1:** cry, dry, my, why **Group 2:** furry, city, happy, funny Have the students read the words in group 1 aloud and clap for each one. How many times did you clap for each word? (1) If you only clap once for each word, the word has one word part called a **syllable**. Have the sudents say and clap for each word in Group 2. How many word parts or syllables does each word have? (2) Listen to each word that I say. Tell us how many syllables are in the word and what the letter 'y' says. **Words:** 1. buy (y says i; one syllable) 2. shy (y says i; one syllable) 3. spy (y says i; one syllable) What can you tell us about a word that ends with 'y' that says 'i?' (If a word has only one syllable, the letter 'y' makes the long 'i' vowel sound.) Listen to these words: funny, forty, city, furry. What letter does each word end with? (y) What sound does the letter 'y' make? (the long 'e' sound) How many word parts are in each word? (2) Listen to each word that I say and tell us the sound the letter 'y' makes in each one. **Words:** 1. family (long e) 2. pry (long i) 3. scurry (long e) 4. guy (long i) 5. happy (long e) 6. buy (long i)

Activity Work Sheet: Page 81 Students are to say each word and record the number of syllables and the vowel sound that the 'y' makes in each one. **Answer Key:** 1. bunny; 2, long e 2. fly; 1, long i 3. fairy: 2, long e 4. buy 1, long i 5. shy, 1, long i 6. penny, 2, long e 7. why, 1, long i 8. happy, 2, long e 9. funny, 2, long e 10. lady, 2, long e

Day 3: Review the 'y' as long 'i' and 'y' as long 'e.' Use the following riddles. 1. I tell how someone feels. It is a good feeling. It ends with a 'y' that sounds like a long 'e.' (happy) 2. I am a sweet treat. Bees make me. I end with a 'y' that has the long 'e' sound. (honey) 3. I am something you do in a plane. I end with a 'y' that has the long 'i' sound. (fly) 4. I am a red flower that grows in fields. I make you remember soldiers who died in wars. I end with a 'y' that has the long 'e' sound. (poppy) 5. This words tells what people do in stores. It ends with a 'y' that makes the long 'i' sound. (buy)

Activity Worksheet: Page 82 Students are to classify the words in the correct columns. Answer Key: Column 1: penny, bunny, hurry, lady, money, honey, happy Column 2: dry, shy, sky, try, fly, fry, sly

Day 4: Review the sounds that the letter 'y' makes as vowels and as a consonant. Record the following words on a chart: yellow, lady, shy, yard, dry, yawn, hurry, furry, my. Have the students classify the words under the following headings: 'y' as long 'e'; 'y' as long 'i'; 'y' as a consonant.

Activity Worksheet: Page 83 Have the students classify each sentence to the picture it is describing. Pictures: 1. cry 2. money 3. hockey 4. sky 5. fly 6. puppy 7. pony 8. fairy Answer Key: 4, 8, 3, 2, 5, 6, 1, 7

Day 5: Auditory Test on the Sounds Made By the Letter 'Yy' Page 84
Look at the letters in each box. Listen to the word that I say. Circle the sound that you hear the letter 'Yy' make in each word. Is it the long vowel 'e' or 'i' or the consonant 'y?' **Words:** 1. lady 2. guy 3. yard 4. sunny 5. yellow 6. try 7. furry 8. yarn 9. my 10. family Answer Key: 1. e 2. i 3. y 4. e 5. y 6. i 7. e 8. y 9. i 10. e

Visual Discrimination Test on the Sounds Made by the Letter 'Yy'
Picture Key: Row 1: bunny, cry, yak, fly Row 2: happy, sky, yoyo, yard Row 3: twenty, spy, yarn, puppy
The students will circle the sound made by the letter 'y' in each picture. **Answer Key:** Row 1: long e; long i; Yy; long i Row 2: long e, long i, Yy, Yy Row 3: long e, long i, Yy, long e

SSR1141 ISBN: 9781771586870

Name: _____ Day 1 | Week 13

The letter 'y' can make **two** vowel sounds.

It can say the **long 'i'** sound as in '**try**' or the **long 'e'** sound as in the word '**happy.**'

Say each picture's name and listen for the sound that the letter 'y' makes.

Is it the **long 'i'** sound or the **long 'e'** sound?
Print the name of the sound on the **line** under each picture. **Example:** long e; long i

The letter 'y' can say the long 'i' sound or the long 'e' sound in words

Name: _____   Day 2 | Week 13

A **syllable** can be a **word** or **part** of a word.

If a word ends with a '**y**' that makes the **long 'i'** sound, it will have **one** syllable.

Examples: buy, my, why, try

Words that end with the **long vowel 'e'** sound will have **two** syllables.

Examples: funny, happy, tricky, sticky

Say the word in each box. **Print** the number of syllables that you hear and the sound that the '**y**' makes in each one.

Words	Syllables	Sound 'Yy' Makes
1. bunny	_____	_____
2. fly	_____	_____
3. fairy	_____	_____
4. buy	_____	_____
5. shy	_____	_____
6. penny	_____	_____
7. why	_____	_____
8. happy	_____	_____
9. funny	_____	_____
10. lady	_____	_____

Name: _____ Day 3 | Week 13

A word that ends with the letter 'y' that makes the **long 'e'** sound will have **one** syllable.

Examples: why, by, my

A word that ends with the letter 'y' that makes the **long 'i'** sound will have **two** syllables.

Examples: baby, forty, hurry

Read the words in the **Word Box**. **Print** each word in the box that tells the sound that the letter 'y' makes.

Word Box						
penny	dry	shy	bunny	hurry	sly	happy
money	try	fly	honey	sky	lady	fry

'y' makes the long 'e' sound	'y' makes the long 'i' sound
_____	_____
_____	_____
_____	_____
_____	_____
_____	_____
_____	_____
_____	_____

Name: _____   Day 4 | Week 13

Here are some sentences for you to read.
Can you **match** each sentence to the picture that it is talking about?
Record the **number** of the picture on the line at the beginning of each sentence.

1.	2.	3.	4.
5.	6.	7.	8.

___ 1. The sky was filled with fluffy clouds.

___ 2. A fairy can do good things with her wand.

___ 3. The hockey player took the puck down the ice.

___ 4. How much money do you have in your piggy bank?

___ 5. The big, black fly landed on my cookie.

___ 6. The little puppy liked to play with a big bone.

___ 7. I cry when I am sad and afraid.

___ 8. At the farm, I like to ride the little white pony.

Name: _____ Day 5 | Week 13

A. Auditory Test on the Sounds Made by the Letter 'Yy'

1. e i y	2. e i y	3. e i y	4. e i y	5. e i y
6. e i y	7. e i y	8. e i y	9. e i y	10. e i y

B. Visual Discrimination Test on the Sounds Made by the Letter 'Yy'

Week 14: Initial Consonant Blends: sl, st, sk, sp, sm, sn, sw

Objective: To teach the recognition of the two letter blends sl, st, sk, sp, sm, sn, sw and how to use them to identify new words.

Day 1: Introduce the 's' blends 'sl, st, sk and sm' using the following groups of words. Listen to the beginning of each word that I say. **Group 1 Words:** slow, slap, slip, slept, slump What two sounds begin each word? (sl) Record the 'sl' blend on a chart. Repeat the same procedure using the following groups of words. **Group 2 Words:** stove, step, stand, sting, study Record the 'st' blend on the chart. **Group 3 Words:** skinny, skill, skid, skirt, skip. Record 'sk' blend on the chart. **Group 4 Words:** smile, smell, smooth, small, smash Record the 'sm' blend on the chart. How are these words the same? (They all begin with a blend.) What is the first letter in each blend? ('s') What is different in each blend? (The second letter is different.) These letters are called 's' blends. They are usually found at the beginning of words.

Picture Key: Row 1: sled, smoke, sky, stick Row 2: skunk, smell, slippers, stairs Row 3: stool, smile, skates, sleep Row 4: skeleton, stars, skirt, skis

Activity Worksheet: Page 86 The students will record the 's' blend that each picture begins with on the line in each box. **Answer Key:** Row 1: sl, sm, sk, st Row 2: sk, sm, sl, st Row 3: st, sm, sk, sl Row 4: sk, st, sk, sk

Day 2: Introduce the 's' blends 'sp, sn, and sw' using the following groups of words. Listen to the beginning of each word that I say. **Group 1:** snap, sneak, sniff, snore What two sounds does each word begin with? (sn) Record the blend on a chart. Repeat the same process using the following groups of words. **Group 2:** space, speak, spin, spill Record 'sp' on the chart. **Group 3:** sweep, swim, swallow, swoop. Record 'sw' on the chart. How are these words similar? (They begin with a blend.) What letter is repeated in each blend? (s) How is each blend different? (the second letter is different) These blends belong to a big family called the 's' blends.

Picture Key: Row 1: spool, snowman, sweater, spider Row 2: snail, swing, spoon, swan Row 3: swim, spinning wheel, sponge, snake

Activity Worksheet: Page 87 The students are to record the 's' blend that is heard at the beginning of each picture on the line in each box. **Answer Key:** Row 1: sp, sn, sw, sp Row 2: sn, sw, sp, sw Row 3: swim, spinning wheel, sponge, snake

Day 3: Review the 's' **blend** family of sounds using the following activity. On a chart record the '**s**' blends **sl, sk, sm, sn, sp, st,** and **sw**. Have the students locate the blend on the chart that each word said begins with. **Words:** stop, swallow, skin, smash, sliver, sneeze, speak, snack, swirl, skirt, stove, smoke, sleeve

Picture Key: Row 1: skis, swing, stump, smile Row 2: sled, snowball, spool, snake

Activity Worksheet: Page 88 The students are to record '**s**' blends to complete the words below the pictures and then record the words in the sentences. **Picture Answer Key:** Row 1: sk, sw, st, sm Row 2: sl, sn, sp, sn **Sentences:** 1. spool 2. smile 3. stump 4. snake 5. snowball 6. sled 7. skis 8. swing

Day 4: Review the 's' blends by having the students complete the following word endings that are printed on a chart. **Word Endings:** ___ ake, ___ ell, ___ eep, ___ oke, ___ op, ___ ate, ___ ar, ___ iff, ___ oon, ___ eep Possible answers: sn, sp, sl, sm, st, sk, st, sn, sp, sl

Activity Worksheet: Page 89 The students will select the correct word to complete each sentence. **Answer Key:** 1. snack 2. sweep 3. slate 4. smell 5. skip 6. score 7. skit 8. swing 9. stack 10. scare

Day 5: A. Auditory Test on the 'S' Blends sl, sm, st, sk, sw, sn, sp Page 90
The students are to listen to each word that you say and then circle the 's' blend in the numbered boxes.
Words: 1. steam 2. skirt 3. swollen 4. smelly 5. slump 6. sniff 7. sponge 8. smooth **Answer Key:** Circled Blends: 1. st 2. sk 3. sw 4. sm 5. sl 6. sn 7. sp 8. sm

B. Visual Discrimination Test on the 'S' Blends sl, sm, sn, sk, sw, sn, sp
The students are to complete each sentence with a word from the Word Box. **Answer Key:** 1. skull 2. swim 3. steep 4. sleigh 5. smoke 6. sneak 7. spear 8. snore 9. spent 10. sweet

SSR1141 ISBN: 9781771586870   85   © On The Mark Press

Name: _____ Day 1 | Week 14

A **blend** is made of two letters.

It is found most of the time at the beginning of a word.

Some blends begin with an '**s**' which is followed by a different consonant

In the '**s**' blend family you will find '**sl**, **st**, **sk**, and **sm**.'

Print the '**s**' blend that you hear at the beginning of each picture on the line in each box.

Does it begin with '**sl**, **st**, **sk**, or **sm**?'

___ed	___oke	___y	___ick
___unk	___ell	___ippers	___airs
___ool	___ile	___ates	___eep
___eleton	___ars	___irt	___is

Name: _____ Day 2 | Week 14

The 's' blend family is a large one.

In the 's' blend family you will find '**sp, sn,** and **sw**' too.

Examples: **sp**in, **sn**ap, **sw**eet

Print the 's' blend that you hear in each picture on the line in each box.

Does it begin with '**sp**, **sn**, or **sw**?'

 ___ool	 ___owman	 ___eater	 ___ider
 ___ail	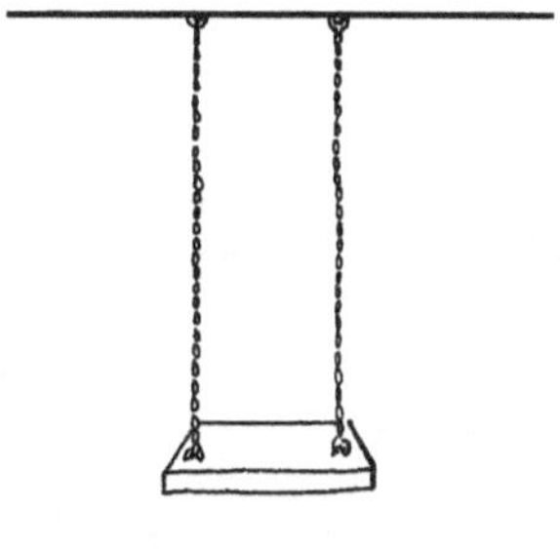 ___ing	 ___oon	 ___an
 ___im	 ___inning	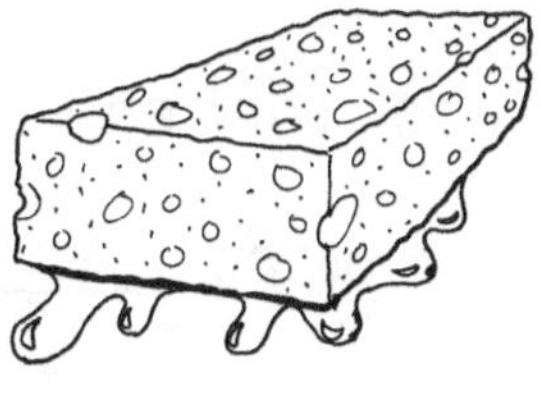 ___onge	 ___ake

Name: _____   Day 3 | Week 14

The 's' blend family has seven sounds.

They are **sk**, **sl**, **sm**, **sn**, **sp**, **st**, and **sw**.

These word begin many words. Practise using them with the following exercises.

Print the blend heard at the beginning of each picture on the line to complete its name. Use these words to **complete** the sentences under the pictures.

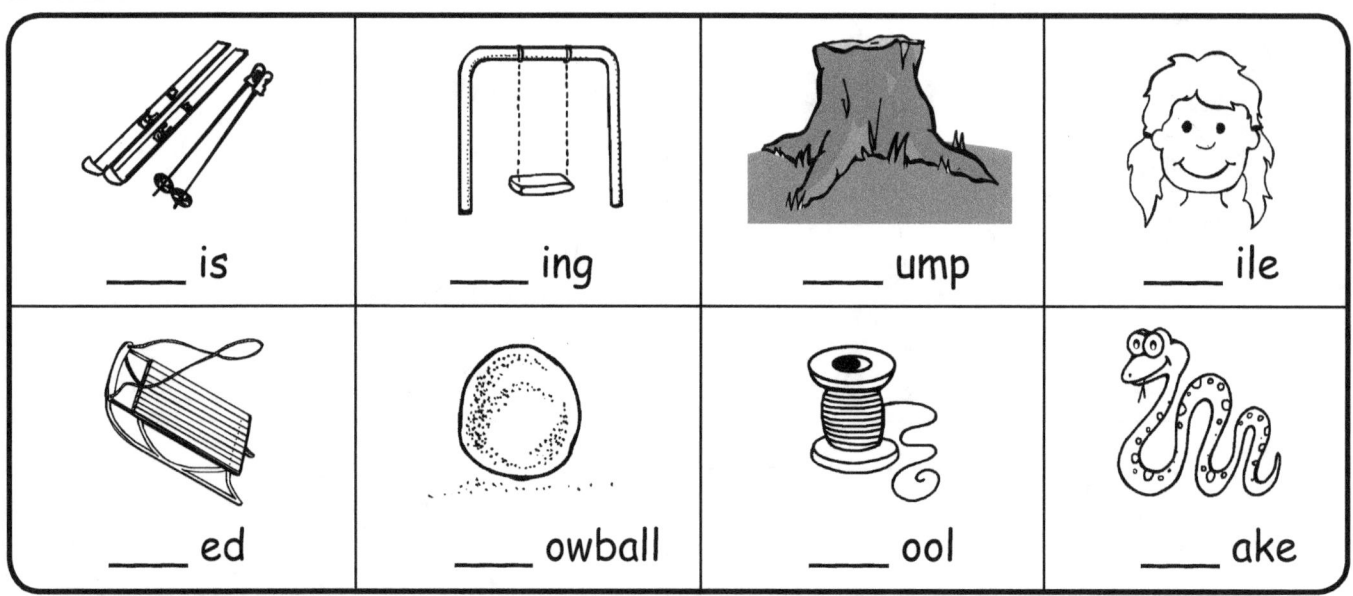

___ is   ___ ing   ___ ump   ___ ile

___ ed   ___ owball   ___ ool   ___ ake

1. My mother used blue thread from a _____ to fix my jeans.

2. The little girl had a big _____ on her face when she won the race.

3. The chipmunk made its home in an old tree _____.

4. The little garter _____ wiggled very fast to get across the grass.

5. The boys made a snowfort and had a _____ fight.

6. The children rode in a dog _____ across the snow to their home.

7. _____ are used to go down a hill quickly.

8. I like to go up high on a _____ to see the sky.

Name: _____   Day 4 | Week 14

Many words begin with the 's' blends 'sl, sm, sn, st, sk, sw and sp.'

Complete each sentence below with the correct word that begins with a 's' blend.

1. I like to eat green grapes for a _____ at school.
   (stack, snack, smack)

2. I had to _____ all the dirt on the floor into a pile.
   (sleep, sweep, steep)

3. Many years ago, children at school used a _____ to write on.
   (skate, state, slate)

4. A skunk sprays a bad _____ when it is afraid.
   (spell, smell, swell)

5. At school, I like to _____ with my friends at recess.
   (slip, snip, skip)

6. What is the _____ of the boys' hockey game?
   (snore, score, store)

7. The children played in a _____ about The Three Bears.
   (slit, spit, skit)

8. At the park, I like to play on a _____ and go down the slide.
   (swing, sting, sling)

9. The tall _____ of books fell all over the floor with a big bang.
   (snack, smack, stack)

10. The little ghost loved to _____ people who came into the old house.
    (stare, spare, scare)

Name: _____ Day 5 | Week 14

A. Auditory Test on the 's' blends 'sl, sm, st, sk, sw, sn, sp'

1.	st	sl	sn	sm	2.	st	sl	sn	sm
	sk	sw	sp			sk	sw	sp	
3.	st	sl	sn	sm	4.	st	sl	sn	sm
	sk	sw	sp			sk	sw	sp	
5.	st	sl	sn	sm	6.	st	sl	sn	sm
	sk	sw	sp			sk	sw	sp	
7.	st	sl	sn	sm	8.	st	sl	sn	sm
	sk	sw	sp			sk	sw	sp	

B. Visual Discrimination Test on the 's' blends 'sl, sm, st, sk, sw, sn, sp'

Word Box

sleigh   smoke   steep   swim   sneak   spear   sweet   skull   snore   spent

1. The bone in your head is called your _____.

2. Every day when it is hot I like to _____ in our pool.

3. The men had to climb a very _____, rocky hill.

4. Santa's _____ is pulled by eight reindeer and Rudolph.

5. We knew the house was on fire when we saw the _____.

6. I watched the fox _____ around the henhouse looking for hens.

7. The hunter threw a _____ at the lion and killed it.

8. I heard my father _____ when he was sleeping.

9. I went to the store and _____ some money on toys.

10. Candy is a very _____ treat.

Week 15: Initial Consonant Blends 'bl, cl, fl, gl, pl, sl'

Objective: To teach the recognition and usage of the two letter 'l' blends **'bl, cl, fl, gl, pl, sl.'**

Day 1: Record the following words on a chart. **Words:** black, cluck, flat, glad, play, slap Look at this group of words. In what way do the words look the same? (They all have the letter 'l' after the first letter. Have the students say the words aloud. What did you notice about the two beginning letters in each word? (You can hear the sound made by the first and second letters together.)What are the names of the two letters at the beginning of each word. List the blends on the chart as the students respond. (**Blends:** bl, cl, fl, gl, pl, sl) These letters are called **'l'** blends and are seen at the beginning of many words.

Picture Key: Row 1: flag, plate, sled, plane Row 2: globe, block, cloud, fly Row 3: clown, glue, blow, slide

Activity Worksheet: Page 92 The students are to complete each word with the correct blend to match each picture. Answer Key: Row 1: fl, pl, sl, pl Row 2: gl, bl, cl, fl Row 3: cl, gl, bl, sl

Day 2: Review the 'l' blends with the following exercise. **Riddles:** 1. I am a fruit. Sometimes I am purple or green. I begin with 'pl.' (plum) 2. I am part of a shirt or jacket. I cover your arms. I begin with 'sl.' (sleeves) 3. I am a kind of map. I am shaped like a ball. I begin with 'gl.' (globe) 4. I am used when it is dark. I help look for something or someone. I begin with 'fl.' (flashlight) 5. I am red in colour. I travel throughout your body. I begin with 'bl.' (blood) 6. I am a small room. Things are stored inside me. I begin with 'cl.' (closet)

Picture Key: Row 1: blocks, glass, clown, plate Row 2: sled, flag, plane, clap

Activity Worksheet: Page 93 The students are to spell the word that matches each picture and to print it on the line. The words are to be used to complete each sentence. **Answer Key:** <u>Pictures:</u> Row 1: blocks, glass, clown, plate Row 2: sled, flag, plane, clap <u>Sentences:</u> 1. glass 2. plate 3. clap 4. plane 5. flag 6. blocks 7. sled 8. clown

Day 3: Review the 'l' blends with the following activity. Record the 'l' blends at the top of a chart. Below the blends record the following word endings. 1. __ug 2. __ink 3. __ear 4. __ick 5. __ind 6. __ap 7. __ow 8. __ad 9. __op 10. __ap The students are to complete each word ending with an 'l' blend that answers each clue. **Clues and Answers:** 1. used in a switch plate (plug) 2. to make your eyelids move quickly (blink) 3. can see through (clear) 4. the sound a door makes when it closes (click) 5. cannot see (blind) 6. to hit someone with your hand (slap) 7. Some bugs do this at night. (glow) 8. to be happy (glad) 9. to fall down quickly (flop) 10. the way a bird moves its wings (flap)

Activity Worksheet: Page 94 The students are to circle **'l' blends** in the word search and then print them beside their meainings. **Answer Key:** <u>Words in the Word Search:</u> clay, plenty, flame, float, sleigh, blanket, gleam, slam, flip **Meanings:** 1. clay 2. class 3. blanket 4. float 5. sleigh 6. slam 7. gleam 8. flame 9. plenty 10. flip

Day 4: Review the 'l' blends with these riddles: 1. I begin with 'fl' and I am a group of birds. (flock) 2. I am a part of a house. You walk on me every day. I begin with fl. (floor) 3. I am a sticky liquid. I make things stick together. I begin with gl. (glue) 4. You should use me every day on your teeth. I begin with 'fl.' (floss) 5. It is a very bad snowstorm. No one can travel far. It begins with 'bl.'(blizzard) 6. It is a sound that a hen makes. It begins with 'cl.' (cluck) 7. I am used to stop water running out of a sink or bathtub. I begin with 'pl.' (plug) 8. You can do this on ice. It begins with 'sl.' (slide)

Activity Worksheet: Page 95 The students are to spell the word under its picture and then print the correct word in each sentence. **Answer Key:** <u>Pictures:</u> Row 1: bluejay, clam, sleep, glass, plum Row 2: flake, clover, blowing, clock, blocks <u>Sentences:</u> 1. slink 2. clop, 3. flow 4. blink 5. sling 6. blow 7. clap 8. flap 9. flock 10. clump

Day 5: A. Auditory Test on the 'l' blends: Page 96
The teacher will say a 'word' for each box. The students will circle the 'l' blend heard at its beginning. **Words** 1. flare 2. planet 3. slump 4. glide 5. closet 6. blossom 7. clover 8. blister **Answer Key:** Sounds to be circled: 1. fl 2. pl 3. sl 4. gl 5. cl 6. bl 7. cl 8. bl

B. Visual Discrimination Test on the 'l' Blends:
The students will use 'l' blends to complete the words in the sentences. **Answer Key:** 1. flames, place 2. plow, plant 3. slice, plate 4. blind, block 5. clouds, blizzard 6. glue, floor 7. player, flash 8. sleeves, blue 9. claws, black 10. flowers, bloom

SSR1141 ISBN: 9781771586870 © On The Mark Press

Name: _____   Day 1 | Week 15

The 'L' Blend Family
bl, cl, fl, gl, pl, sl

You have met another family of sounds.

This family is called the **'l' blend** family.

In this family live the sounds that '**bl, cl, fl, gl, pl,** and **sl**' make.

Does the picture in each box begin with '**bl, cl, fl, gl, pl or sl?**

Print the blend on the line to make the word for each picture.

 ___ag	 ___ate	 ___ed	 ___ane
 ___obe	 ___ock	 ___oud	 ___y
 ___own	 ___ue	 ___ow	 ___id

Name: _____   Day 2 | Week 15

Knowing the 'l' blend family helps you to read and spell words.

Example: blind, blend, blow
         clip, clop, clap

Spell the word for each picture. Match each word to its sentence.

1. I like to drink a _____ of milk when I eat.

2. Put the cookies on a _____ to have as a snack.

3. Let's _____ our hands when we sing the song.

4. Flying in a _____ is a fast way to travel to a far away place.

5. Canada's _____ is red and white and has a red maple leaf on it.

6. Children like to build things with lots of _____.

7. The children on the _____ zoomed down the big, snowy hill.

8. The funny _____ made all the boys and girls laugh.

Name: _____   Day 3 | Week 15

Look for 'l' **blend words** in the Word Search.
Circle each one.
Match each 'l' blend to its meaning.

```
a b c d e f g h i j k l m n o p y
q r s t c l a y b n u c l a s s p
a b c h j o p l e n t y u i o p i
u v b r t y i o p b n m f l i p n
n m f l a m e t y b n u v i n m p
y b g h f l o a t v b n m o m k v
d f g m u i o s t s l e i g h n m
y u i o p h j g f d e v h n j m r
o p n m b l a n k e t m o p r s m
z g l e a m h j o i m k o p r t q
d f h y m k l o p t y s l a m a b
```

Meanings:

1. a kind of mud _____

2. a group of children at school _____

3. it keeps you warm at night _____

4. boats do this on water _____

5. used for travelling in the winter _____

6. to shut a door quickly _____

7. to shine brightly _____

8. seen in a fire _____

9. to have a lot of things _____

10. to turn over _____

Name: _____   Day 4 | Week 15

Let's see how well you know and can use the blends in the **'l' blend** family.

Spell each word on the line under the picture.

Print the missing word on the line in each sentence.

1. I saw the fox _____ away carrying a chicken. (clink, blink, slink)

2. The horse's feet went clip _____ down the street. (flop, slop, clop)

3. In the spring, rivers _____ very quickly. (flow, slow, glow)

4. The hot, bright sun made my eyes _____. (clink, blink, slink)

5. The boy had to wear a _____ on his broken arm. (cling, sling, fling)

6. I can _____ a big bubble with my gum. (slow, blow, glow)

7. The clown made the children _____ their hands. (flap, slap, clap)

8. I watched the robin _____ its wings and fly away. (clap, slap, flap)

9. The boy had to look after a _____ of sheep. (clock, flock, block)

10. The rabbit hid behind a _____ of bushes. (slump, plump, clump)

Name: _____ Day 5 | Week 15

A. Auditory Test on the 'l' Blends

1. bl cl fl gl pl sl	5. bl cl fl gl pl sl
2. bl cl fl gl pl sl	6. bl cl fl gl pl sl
3. bl cl fl gl pl sl	7. bl cl fl gl pl sl
4. bl cl fl gl pl sl	8. bl cl fl gl pl sl

B. Visual Discrimination Test on the 'l' Blends

1. The ____ames in the fire____ace made the room warm and cozy.

2. In the spring, a farmer will ____ow his fields and ____ant hay and corn.

3. I want a big ____ice of chocolate cake on my ____ate.

4. The ____ind man walked with a cane around the ____ock.

5. The dark ____ouds told us a ____izzard was coming.

6. Who spilled the ____ue all over the ____oor?

7. Billy is a hockey ____ayer who can move as quick as a ____ash on skates.

8. The ____eeves on my ____ue coat are too short.

9. An eagle has long, sharp ____aws and ____ack feathers.

10. In the spring, the ____owers will ____oom

Week 16: Initial Consonant Blends 'br, cr, dr, fr, gr, pr, tr'

Objective: To introduce and reinforce the recall and usage of the 'r' blends

Day 1: Introduce the consonant blends **br, cr, dr**, and **fr** using the following sentences. Record 'br, cr, dr, and tr' on a chart leaving room to record words under each one. Sentences: 1. Brutus the Brontosaurus bravely crossed the broken bridge. Record the 'br' words on the chart. 2. Droofus the Dragon dreamed that he was a drummer who played a big drum in a dragon band. 3. Crocus the Crab was a creature who crawled into cracks to hide. 4. Freddie is a green frog with brown freckles on his body who loves to frighten and eat insects. Discuss the words on the chart. How are all of these words the same. (The second letter in each word is the letter 'r.') This group of sounds belong to the 'r' blend family. Have the students read the words in each sentence and circle the initial blend.

Picture Key: Row 1: dragon, fridge, bread, drum Row 2: broom, crown, crayons, frame

Activity Worksheet: Page 98 The students are to complete each picture word with an 'r' blend and then use the words to complete each sentence. **Picture Answer Key:** Row 1: dr, fr, br, dr Row 2: br, cr, cr, fr **Sentence Answer Key:** 1. dragon 2. fridge 3. bread 4. crown 5. crayons 6. frame 7. broom 8. drum

Day 2: Introduce the consonant blends '**gr, tr,** and **pr**' using the following sentences. Record '**gr, tr,** and **pr**' on a chart leaving room to record words under each one from the following sentences. **Sentences:** 1. Grasshopper Green lives in a big field where grain grows and he can hop great distances on the growing grain. 2. Tracey Triceratops tramped along the trail trying to find a treat to eat. 3. The prince proudly saved the princess from the soldier on his prancing horse.

Picture Key: Row 1: triangle, grapes, present, grass Row 2: truck, princess, grin, tree

Activity Worksheet: Page 99 The students are to complete picture words with an 'r' blend and then use the words to complete each sentence. **Picture Key:** Row 1: triangle, grapes, present, grass, Row 2: truck, princess, grin, tree **Sentence Answers:** 1. grass 2. present 3. grapes 4. triangle 5. truck 6. tree 7. grin 8. princess

Day 3: Review the '**r**' blends. Record the following words on a chart and have the students tell what they say. **Words:** 1. look, crook, brook 2. made, trade, grade 3. guess, press, dress 4. down, frown, drown 5. sand, brand, grand 5. bank, crank, prank 6. hush, brush, crush 7. room, broom, groom 8. sick, brick, prick

Activity Worksheet: Page 100 Students will choose the correct words from the 'R' Blend Word Box to complete each sentence. **Answer Key:** 1. crab, brown 2. branch, tree 3. dream, dragon 4. frown, cry 5. grain, grew 6. frog, prince, princess 7. trunk, drum, train 8. brick, broke

Day 4: Review students' word attack skills with this exercise. Record these words on a chart: braids, crawl, drain, greedy, trout, print, trash, brain. Which word on the chart means 1. to eat or to want lots (greedy) 2. a hair style (braids) 3. to move low on the floor (crawl) 4. water goes down it (drain) 5. used for thinking (brain) 6. a kind of fish (trout) 7. garbage (trash) 8. done with a pencil on paper (print)

Activity Worksheet: Page 101 Students are to circle words that begin with 'r' blends in the word search. They are to match the words to their meanings. **Word Search Words:** bread, drawing, drowsy, tractor, crayon, cradle, grasshopper, pretty, broom, trumpet **Meanings:** 1. bread 2. drowsy 3. crayon 4. grasshopper 5. broom 6. pretty 7. cradle 8. tractor 9. drawing 10. trumpet

Day 5: Auditory Test on the 'r' blends 'br, cr, dr, fr, gr, pr, tr' Page 102
The students are to listen to each word said by the teacher and circle the 'r' blend in the numbered boxes. **Words:** 1. creature 2. pretzal 3. tremble 4. frighten 5. grand 6. drapes 7. brother 8. greedy **Answer Key:** Circled 'r' blends: 1. cr 2. pr 3. tr 4. fr 5. gr 6. dr 7. br 8. gr

Visual Discrimination Test on the 'r' blends 'br, cr, dr, fr, gr, pr, tr'
The students are to complete each sentence with a word from the Word Box. **Answer Key:** 1. braids 2. drank 3. grin 4. Frosty 5. treat 6. prickly 7. creep 8. crickets 9. branch 10. trail

SSR1141 ISBN: 9781771586870 97 © On The Mark Press

Name: _____ Day 1 | Week 16

The 'r' blend family has **seven** sounds.

Today we are going to talk about **four** of the sounds.

They are **br**, **cr**, **dr**, and **gr**.

Complete the word for each picture using one of the four sounds.

Welcome to the 'R' blend family!

____agon ____idge ____ead ____um

____oom ____own ____ayons ____ame

Complete each sentence with a **picture word**.

1. The bad _____ liked to burn things with his fire.

2. Put the milk in the _____ to keep it cold.

3. I can smell _____ baking in the oven.

4. The king wore a _____ made of gold and shiny stones.

5. Use your _____ and neatly colour the pictures.

6. My mother put my school picture in a shiny gold _____.

7. Use the _____ to sweep the kitchen floor.

8. The boy banged on the big _____ to make a loud sound.

Name: _____ Day 2 | Week 16

There are more members of the 'r' blend family.

They are 'gr, tr, and pr.'

Complete the word for each picture using the blends 'gr, tr, and pr.'

Welcome to the 'R' Blend Family

br cr dr
fr gr pr
    tr

___ iangle   ___ apes   ___ esent   ___ ass

___ uck   ___ incess   ___ in   ___ ee

Complete each sentence with the correct picture word.

1. In the spring the rain makes the _____ turn green.

2. Under the Christmas tree sat a very big _____ for a little boy.

3. Purple and green _____ grow on vines.

4. A _____ is a shape that has three sides and three points.

5. The big _____ ran through a puddle and I got splashed.

6. The squirrel climbed the _____ and hid its nut in a hole.

7. The little boy had a _____ on his face when he won first prize.

8. The _____ found a frog that turned into a prince.

Name: _____   Day 3 | Week 16

Knowing the 'r' blends helps you to sound out and spell many words.

In the 'r' blend family there is '**br, cr, dr, fr, gr, pr** and **tr**.'

Choose the correct words that begin with 'r' blends to complete each sentence.

Welcome to the 'R' Blend Family

br	cr	dr
fr	gr	pr
tr		

Word Box

brick   train   broke   prince   cry   trunk   frog   drum   grain   dream
grew   frown   branch   brown   crab   dragon   tree   brick   princess

1. The little _____ walked slowly on the _____ sand.

2. The robin made her nest on a _____ of a maple _____.

3. I had a bad _____ last night about a _____.

4. The unhappy boy had a _____ on his face and began to _____.

5. The _____ in the big field _____ tall quickly.

6. The _____ turned into a _____ and surprised the _____.

7. In the old _____ we found an old toy _____ and a toy _____.

8. Someone threw a _____ and _____ our big window.

SSR1141 ISBN: 9781771586870   100   © On The Mark Press

Name: _____   Day 4 | Week 16

Look in the word search and **circle** all the words that begin with an 'r' blend.

Match the circled words to their meanings.

Print each word on the line beside its meaning.

```
b c d g h j y k l m n o p q r s t c v g u m x r o u p u a
b r e a d i o u t r b d r a w i n g o p r s t b r o o m x
k j k n m d r o w s y n m b g f d s r t r a c t o r m l o
m h j b k c r a y o n n b m l c x z c r a d l e m p o w
w e r t o p l m n b v f g d c x z w e r s t u v w x z m n
g r a s s h o p p e r b n c v d g f e w t y u i o p l m v
a b c f t r e w p r e t t y o p n j k l m n o p q r s t u
s d f g h j k l t r u m p e t n k o p u y t r e w q b n m
```

1. made from flour _____

2. sleepy _____

3. used to colour a picture _____

4. a big bug that hops and spits _____

5. used for sweeping _____

6. nice to look at _____

7. a baby's first bed _____

8. used to pull a plow _____

9. a kind of picture _____

10. used to make music _____

Name: _____ Day 5 | Week 16

A. Auditory Test on the 'r' blends 'br, cr, dr, fr, gr, tr, pr'

1. br cr dr fr gr pr tr	2. br cr dr fr gr pr tr
3. br cr dr fr gr pr tr	4. br cr dr fr gr pr tr
5. br cr dr fr gr pr tr	6. br cr dr fr gr pr tr
7. br cr dr fr gr pr tr	8. br cr dr fr gr pr tr

B. Visual Discrimination Test on the 'r' blends 'br, cr, dr, fr, gr, pr, tr

Word Box

crickets   Frosty   braids   treat   prickly   grin   creep   branch   drank   trail

1. The lady put _____ in the little girl's hair.

2. The horse _____ all of the water in the pail.

3. The little boy had a happy _____ on his face.

4. There is a song about a snowman called _____.

5. My grandfather bought me a _____ at the candy store.

6. A porcupine has a _____ coat made of quills.

7. The baby boy liked to _____ all over the floor.

8. At night the _____ like to sing songs to each other.

9. The boy tried to swing on the _____ of a tree but fell onto the ground.

10. We walked on a _____ that took us to a big lake.

Week 17: **Initial and Final Digraphs 'sh, ch, th, wh'**

Objective: To teach students that words begin and end with the digraphs 'sh, ch, wh, and th.'

Day 1: Introduce the digraphs '**sh, ch, wh,** and **th**' in the initial position using the following sentences. Discuss the words in each sentence and the digraph that begins most of the words in each sentence. **Sentence #1:** Shannon, a shepherd, sheared his shaggy sheep in a shack. Discuss the digraphs that are heard at the beginning of the underlined words. Print the words on a chart. Underline the digraph and discuss the sound it makes. Repeat the same process for the digraphs in the following sentences. **Sentence #2:** Charlie, a cheeky chipmunk chattered at a chickadee and chased it from his tree. **Sentence #3:** The three thieves thought they could steal thousands of dollars from the theatre. **Sentence #4:** The whale whacked his whopper of a tail on the wharf.

Picture Key: Row 1: chicken, thimble, wheel, shirt Row 2: church, shoe, thumb, whiskers Row 3: whip, thief, chimney, shovel Row 4: shore, chair, thirty, whistle

Activity Worksheet: Page 104 The students are to complete each word with the correct digraph.
Answer Key: Row 1: ch, th, wh, sh Row 2: ch, sh, th, wh Row 3: wh, th, ch, sh Row 4: sh, ch, th, wh

Day 2: Introduce the digraphs 'sh, ch, and th' in the final position in words. Listen to each group of words that I say and tell me where you hear the sounds 'sh, ch, and th'. **Word Group #1:** fish, crash, push, cash (sh; the end of the word) **Word Group #2:** ranch, pinch, munch (ch; at the end of the word) **Word Group #3:** teeth, bath, south, path (th; at the end of the word) Review the concept using this exercises. What sound do you hear at the end of each word? 1. smooth (th) 2. branch (ch) 3. splash (sh) 4. lunch (ch) 5. birth (th) 6. cash (sh)

Picture Key: Row 1: leash, teeth, couch, dash Row 2: trash, death, moth, match Row 3: torch, mouth, fish, dish Row 4: watch, wreath, branch, brush

Activity Worksheet: Page 105 The students are to record the digraph heard at the end of each word.
Answer Key: Row 1: sh, th, ch, sh Row 2: sh, ch, th, ch Row 3: ch, th, th, sh Row 4: ch, th, ch, sh

Day 3: Review the initial and final position of the digraphs 'sh, ch, th, wh' using the following exercise. Record the digraphs on a chart. **Exercise:** I am going to say a word. You are to listen for the sounds 'sh, ch, wh, th.' You are to tell where you can hear it and which digraph is making the sound. **Words:** 1. shade (sh, beginning) 2. wheeze (wh, beginning) 3. porch (ch, ending) 4. thirsty (th, beginning) 5. whirl (wh, beginning) 6. pinch (ch, ending) 8. splash (sh ending) 9. mouth (th, ending) 10. checkers (beginning, ch)

Picture Key: Row 1: chest, thread, dish, wheel Row 2: shoe, bench, cheek, tooth

Activity Worksheet: Page 106 The students are to complete each word with a digraph. The words made are to be used to complete the sentences. **Answer Key:** Pictures - Row 1: ch, th, sh, wh Row 2: sh, ch, ch, th Sentences: 1. dish 2. cheek 3. wheel 4. thread 5. bench 6. shoe 7. tooth 8. chest

Day 4: Review the initial and final digraphs 'sh, ch, wh, th.' Record the following words on a chart. **Words:** 1. pea(ch) 2. (th) ink 3. (wh) eat 4. (ch) air 5. (sh) ed 6. cra (sh) 7. clo (th) 8. mun (ch) 9. da (sh) 10. (sh) ake Have the students use digraphs to complete the words.

Activity Worksheet: Page 107 The students are to complete each sentence with the correct word.
Answer Key: 1. chum 2. shark 3. thumb 4. whiskers 5. smash 6. match 7. south 8. checkers 9. push 10. shelf

Day 5: Auditory Test on the Initial and Final Digraphs 'sh, ch, wh, th' Page 108 The students are to circle the digraph that they hear at the beginning or ending of each word said by the teacher. Words: 1. shine 2. thirsty 3. whisper 4. chicken 5. flash 6. crutch 7. mouth 8. chin Answer Key: Circled digraphs: 1. sh 2. th 3. wh 4. ch 5. sh 6. ch 7. th 8. ch

Visual Discrimination Test on the Initial and Final Digraphs 'sh, ch, th, wh'
The students are to choose and print the correct word to fit each sentence. **Answer Key:** 1. wheel 2. hatch 3. shell 4. brush 5. path 6. thaw 7. cheer 8. sheet

Name: _____   Day 1 | Week 17

Digraphs are two letter sounds that are heard at the **beginning** of words.

They are '**sh**, **ch**, **th**, and **wh**.'

In each digraph there is the letter 'h.'

Print the sound that you hear at the beginning of each picture word.

___ icken   ___ imble   ___ eel   ___ irt

___ urch   ___ oe   ___ umb   ___ iskers

___ ip   ___ ief   ___ imney   ___ ovel

      30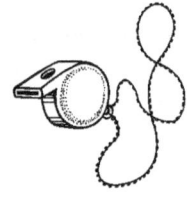
___ ore   ___ air   ___ irty   ___ istle

Name: _____   Day 2 | Week 17

Some digraphs are heard at the **end** of words.
Examples: wa**sh**   pat**ch**   nor**th**
They are '**sh**, **ch**, and **th**.'

Complete the words in the box with the final digraphs '**sh**, **ch**, and **th**.'

Welcome to the Digraph Family

sh ch wh th

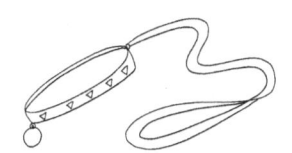  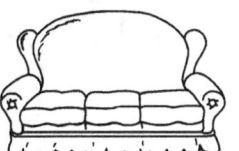 

lea ___   tee ___   cou ___   da ___

tra ___   pea ___   mo ___   mat ___

tor ___   mou ___   fi ___   di ___

   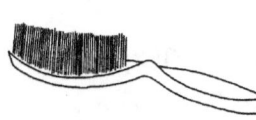

wat ___   wrea ___   bran ___   bru ___

Name: _____   Day 3 | Week 17

Some words begin with '**sh, ch, th,** and **wh**.'

Some words end with '**sh, ch,** and **th**.'

Use the sounds '**sh, ch, wh,** and **th**' to spell the picture words in the box.

___ est   ___ read   di ___   ___ eel

___ oe   ben ___   ___ eek   too ___

Use the words that you made in the sentences.

1. The _____ fell on the floor and broke.

2. The little boy had paint on his _____.

3. The _____ on my bike had a flat tire.

4. Mom used some _____ to fix the hole in my pants.

5. The old man sat on a _____ in the park and fed the birds.

6. I lost my good _____ on the way home from school.

7. I put my _____ under my pillow last night.

8. The old _____ full of toys sat in the attic.

Name: _____   Day 4 | Week 17

Digraphs are **two letter** sounds that are heard at the **beginning** or **ending** of words.

Ch, sh, and **th** are digraphs heard at the end of words.

Examples: push, witch, tooth

Use the words in the **Word Box** to complete each sentence.

Word Box				
shelf	chum	push	south	match
smash	checkers	shark	whiskers	thumb

1. A _____ is a friend that you like to play with often.

2. A _____ swam around our boat for a long time.

3. I cut my _____ when I tried to use a knife.

4. The old man had white _____ on his face.

5. The boy threw a rock to _____ the window.

6. The girl lit the candle with a _____.

7. Some birds fly _____ every autumn.

8. The boys like to play _____ on rainy days.

9. Do not _____ other boys and girls when you line up for school.

10. Put the books on the top _____.

Name: _____ Day 5 | Week 17

A. Auditory Test on the Initial and Final Digraphs 'sh, ch, th, wh'

1. sh ch wh th	2. sh ch wh th
3. sh ch wh th	4. sh ch wh th
5. sh ch wh th	6. sh ch wh th
7. sh ch wh th	8. sh ch wh th

B. Visual Discrimination Test on the Initial and Final Digraphs 'sh, ch, wh, th.'

1. The _____ on the car had a flat tire. (whale, wheel, whirl)

2. The eggs in the robin's nest began to _____. (patch, match, hatch)

3. A clam likes to hide inside its hard _____. (sheep, shell, sheet)

4. The little girl liked to _____ her hair. (hush, brush, crush)

5. The boys walked on a _____ that led to a river. (bath, math, path)

6. In the spring the ice will _____ on the lake. (than, that, thaw)

7. Did you hear the people _____ when your team won the game. (chain, chin, cheer)

8. Draw a picture on this _____ of paper. (sheep, sheet, shed)

Week 18: Digraphs 'ph, gh, ck, ng'

Objective: To develop the recognition of the sounds made by the **digraphs 'ph, gh, ck,** and **ng'**

Day 1: Introduce the digraphs **'ph'** and **'gh'** in the following way. Record on a chart the following sentences. 1. The furry fox ran out of the forest. 2. You can take my photo with your cell phone. 3. The horse drank enough water from the trough. Read sentence 1 with the students. What initial consonant is heard at the beginning of three of the words? (f) Say the words: furry, fox, forest. Read sentence 2. Which two words have letters that make the same sound as the consonant 'f.' (photo, phone) What are the letters? (ph) Read sentence three with your students. Which two words in this sentence have the same sound as the consonant 'f?' (enough, trough) What did you learn today about the consonant 'f' and the digraphs 'ph' and 'gh?' They all make the same sound. Where may you find the initial consonant 'f' in words? (at the beginning of words) Where may you hear the digraphs 'ph' and 'gh?' (They may be heard at the beginning, middle and end of words.)

Picture Key: Row 1: phone, trophy, cough, laugh Row 2: photo, elephant, tough, trough

Activity Worksheet: Page 110 The students are to record the digraph 'ph' or 'gh' to complete the picture words and then use the words to complete the sentences. **Answer Key:** <u>Pictures</u> - Row 1: ph, ph, gh, gh Row 2: ph, ph, gh, gh <u>Sentences:</u> 1. trophy 2. cough 3. laugh 4. phone 5. elephant 6. photo 7. tough 8. trough

Day 2: Introduce the final digraphs **'ck'** and **'ng'** using the following sentences written on a chart. **Sentence #1:** <u>Pack</u> your <u>snack</u> in your <u>black</u> <u>backpack</u>. Underline the words. Have the students read the sentence with you. Discuss the two letters that end each underlined word. How does each word end? (letters 'ck') What sound do the letters 'c' and 'k' make at the end of a word? (kuh) Where else do you see the letters 'c' and 'k' in words? ('c' and 'k' are heard at the beginning and ending of a word as a consonant and they both make the same sound. Where do you see the digraph 'ck' in a word? (at the end of the word) **Sentence #2:** The <u>king</u> likes to <u>sing</u> when he is on a <u>swing</u> in the <u>spring</u>. What do you notice about the underlined words. (They all end with the consonants 'ng.') What sound do you hear 'ng' make? (ng) The digraph 'ng' is usually heard at the end of a word.

Picture Key: Row 1: block, king, truck, ring Row 2: swing, clock, wing, rock

Activity Worksheet: Page 111 The students are to complete each picture word with the digraph 'ck' or 'ng.' The picture words are then used in the correct sentences. **Answer Key:** <u>Pictures:</u> Row 1: ck, ng, ck, ng Row 2: ng, ck, ng, ck <u>Sentences:</u> 1. ring 2. wing 3. rock 4. truck 5. swing 6. clock 7. block 8. king

Day 3: Review the final digraphs **'ph, gh, ck,** and **ng.'** On a chart record the four digraphs. Under the digraphs print the following incomplete words. Have the students complete each word with a digraph. Words: 1. so ___ (ng or ck) 2. ___ one (ph) 3. ba ___ (ck or ng) 4. lau ___ (gh) 5. ta ___ (ck) 6. cou ___ (gh) 7. dol ___ in (ph) 8. stri ___ (ng) 9. ne ___ (ck) 10. gra ___ (ph)

Picture Key: Row 1: photo, sing, laugh, brick Row 2: sock, swing, elephant, flock

Activity Worksheet: Page 112 The students are to complete each picture word with the correct digraph and then use the words in the sentences. **Answer Key:** Pictures - Row 1: photo, sing, laugh, brick Row 2: sock, swing, elephant, flocks **Sentences:** 1. laugh 2. flock 3. photo 4. elephant 5. sock 6. sing 7. swing 8. brick

Day 4: Review the digraphs **ph, gh, ck,** and **ng**. Record the following words on a chart. **Words:** 1. wing 2. tick 3. rough 4. dolphin 5. tack 6. song 7. thick 8. laugh 9. trophy 10. pack Read each of the following clues and have the students locate the word that matches each one. **Clues:** 1. an ocean animal (dolphin) 2. a happy sound (laugh) 3. the sound a clock makes (tick) 4. the opposite to thin (thick) 5. a very small nail (tack) 6. won by a team (trophy) 7. something people sing (song) 8. not smooth (rough). 9. part of a bird's body (wing) 10. putting clothes in a suitcase (pack)

Activity Worksheet: Page 113 The students will select the correct word and print it in the sentence. **Answer Key:** 1. snack 2. laugh 3. sack 4. ring 5. socks 6. sing 7. ring 8. duck 9. puck 10. rough

Day 5: Auditory Test on the Initial, Middle and Final Digraphs ph, gh, ck, ng: Page 114 The students are to circle the digraph that they hear in each word said by the teacher. **Words:** 1. quack 2. bring 3. tough 4. photo 5. stick 6. cough 7. hung 8. graph **Answer Key:** 1. ck 2. ng 3. gh 4. ph 5. ck 6. gh 7. ng 8. ph

Visual Discrimination Test on the Initial, Middle and Final Digraphs ph, gh, ck, ng: The students are to complete each sentence with the correct word that has a digraph. **Answer Key:** 1. sting 2. lock 3. cough 4. phone 5. suck 6. trick 7. sick 8. pick

109

Name: _____ Day 1 | Week 18

A **digraph** is a sound made of **two** letters.

It can be at the **beginning**, in the **middle** or at the **end** of a word.

'**Ph**' and '**gh**' are **digraphs** that make the same sound as the initial consonant '**f**.'

Examples: al**ph**abet, enou**gh**, tou**gh**, **ph**one

Does the picture in each box have the '**f**' sound made by the digraph '**ph**' or '**gh**'? Print the sound '**gh**' or '**ph**' on the line in each word.

___ one   ___ ophy   cou ___   lau ___

___ oto   ele ___ ant   tou ___   trou ___

Print each picture **word** that you made in one of the sentences.

1. My baseball team won a shiny _____ for winning the most games.

2. Cover your mouth with your arm when you _____.

3. The clown's tricks made the children _____.

4. Use your cell _____ to take my picture.

5. The big grey _____ used its trunk to suck up some water.

6. My class had its _____ taken outside the school.

7. The _____ boy liked to pick on others to make them cry.

8. The horses drank all of the water in the _____.

Name: _____   Day 2 | Week 18

A **digraph** is a sound made by **two** letters at the end of a word.

The letters '**ng**' and '**ck**' are **digraphs** heard at the **end** of words.

Examples: pick, pack, peck   song, long, bong

Which **digraph** do you hear at the end of each picture word?
Is it '**ck**' or '**ng?**'

blo ___   ki ___   tru ___   ri ___

sw ___   clo ___   wi ___   ro ___

Print each picture word that you made in **one** of the sentences.

1. I liked the gold _____ with the big red stone the best.

2. The little bird broke its _____ when it hit the wall.

3. The big _____ rolled all the way down the hill.

4. A big _____ can carry many things to stores.

5. How high up can you pump your _____?

6. Did you see the mouse run up to the top of the _____ ?

7. You need one more _____ to make your house.

8. The _____ wore a crown and sat on his throne.

Name: _____   Day 3 | Week 18

Many words have the digraphs '**ph**, **gh**, **ck**, and **ng**'.

They may be at the beginning of a word, the middle of a word, or at the end of a word.

Print the missing digraph to finish each picture word.

Is it '**ph**, **gh**, **ck**, or **ng**.'

___ oto   si ___   lau ___   bri ___

so ___   swi ___   ele ___ ant   flo ___

Print the picture words in the sentences.

1. People _____ when they are happy.

2. The _____ of birds was flying south for the winter.

3. My mother put my school _____ in a nice frame.

4. At the circus, a girl sat on the back of an _____.

5. Look for your _____ under your bed.

6. In December, people like to _____ Christmas songs.

7. My dad made me a _____ that hung from a branch of a tall tree.

8. A _____ fell out of the wall of a house and hit the ground.

Name: _____   Day 4 | Week 18

The digraphs '**ph**, **gh**, **ck**, and **ng**' are heard at the end of many words.

Print the **correct** word in each sentence.

1. I like to eat an apple for a _____ at recess. (sack, stack, snack)

2. A funny story makes my class _____ . (laugh, cough, tough)

3. The big brown _____ was full of lots of potatoes.

    (sick, sack, suck)

4. I had to _____ the doorbell three times before someone opened the door.

    (rang, ring, rung)

5. Anne wore a pair of yellow _____ to school on Wednesday.

    (blocks, rocks, socks)

6. Every morning at school we _____ O Canada. (sing, sang, sung)

7. Did you hear the phone _____ ? (ring, rang, rung)

8. The little _____ liked to swim in the pond all summer long..

    (deck, duck, dock)

9. The team got a goal when the _____ flew into the net.

    (pick, pack, puck)

10. The top of the rock feels very _____ and bumpy.

    (tough, rough, laugh

Name: _____   Day 5 | Week 18

A. Auditory Test on the Initial, Middle and Final Digraphs 'ph, gh, ck, ng'

1. ph gh ck ng	2. ph gh ck ng	3. ph gh ck ng	4. ph gh ck ng
5. ph gh ck ng	6. ph gh ck ng	7. ph gh ck ng	8. ph gh ck ng

B. Visual Discrimination Test on the Initial, Middle, and Final Consonants 'ph, gh, ck, ng'

1. Look out for the bee because it might _____ you. (stung, sting, sing)

2. Do not forget to _____ all the doors at bedtime. (lick, lack, lock)

3. A bad cold can make you _____. (click, cough, clang)

4. The _____ rang for a long time. (bone, cone, phone)

5. An elephant uses its trunk to _____ up water. (suck, sack, sick)

6. The boy wanted to play a _____ on his father. (track, trick, truck)

7. The girl was _____ and had to stay home from school. (sack, suck, sick)

8. The hen liked to _____ up grain with her beak. (pack, peck, pick)

Week 19: Recognition of 'R' Controlled Vowels 'ar, er, ir, or, ur'

Objective: To make students aware that the vowel sounds are sometimes controlled by the letter 'r' and that is the only sound that you may hear at the beginning, in the middle, or at the end of a word.

Day 1: Record the words 'car, bar, far' on a chart. Have the students read the words aloud. What do you notice about the sound at the end of each word? (They end the same way.) What sound do you hear? (r) Do you hear the vowel 'a?' (No) When words end with ar, the 'r' does all the talking and shouts out its name. Record the following words on the chart: arm, ark, art. What sound do you hear at the beginning of each word? (r) Does the 'a' say anything? (No) Sometimes words begin with 'ar.' Record these words on a chart: farm, warm, harm. What sound do you hear in the middle of these words?('r') Sometimes 'ar' is in the middle of words.

Picture Key: Row 1: ark, jar, shark Row 2: star, yard, cart Row 3: car, heart, yarn Row 4: barn, card, arm

Activity Worksheet: Page 116 The students are to record the word, 'beginning, middle or end,' on the line under each picture to indicate where they hear the 'r' in the 'r' controlled words. **Answer Key:** Row 1: beginning, ending, middle Row 2: end, middle, middle Row 3: end, middle, middle Row 4: middle, middle, beginning

Day 2: Introduce the 'or' vowel sound. Record these words on a chart: store, orange, for, door, or. Have the students say the words aloud. What sound do the letters 'or' make in these words. (long 'o' and the sound made by the letter 'r') Where do you hear the 'or' sound in the words? (at the beginning, in the middle, and at the end) Review the 'ar' and 'or' controlled vowel sounds using this game. Record the following words on a chart: farm, horn, jar, horse, art, fork, core, pork. Give each clue and have a student locate the word that answers it. Clues: Which word on the chart is 1. a large animal (horse) 2. a musical instrument (horn) 3. a place to raise animals (farm) 4. a container made of glass (jar) 5. drawings and paintings (art) 6. the middle of an apple (core) 7. used for eating (fork) 8. meat from a pig (pork)

Picture Key: Row 1: store, yarn, fork, car Row 2: shore, cork, park, star

Activity Worksheet: Page 117 Students are to spell words that have the controlled vowels 'ar' and 'or' under the pictures and then use them in the following sentences. **Answer Key:** <u>Pictures</u> - Row 1: store, yarn, fork, car Row 2: shore, cork, park, star <u>Sentences</u> - 1. star 2. yarn 3. cork 4. park 5. car 6. fork 7. shore 8. store

Day 3: Introduce the r-controlled vowels 'ur, er, and ir.' Record the following groups of words on a chart: Group 1: hurt, burn, turn Group 2: water, better, other Group 3: first, dirt, stir Discuss each group of words noting the 'r-controlled vowels' in each group. In group one the vowel 'u' is not heard as it is bossed by the letter 'r' In group two, the letter 'e' is not heard as it is bossed by the letter 'r.' In group three, the letter 'i' is bossed by the letter 'r.' In many words the 'ur and ir' controlled vowels are found inside the word while the 'er' controlled vowel is found mainly at the end of words.

Picture Key: Row 1: letter, turtle, churn, skirt Row 2: turkey, shirt, bird, fir

Activity Worksheet: Page 118 The students are to name the pictures and then use the words in the sentences. **Answer Key:** <u>Pictures</u>- Row 1: letter, turtle, churn, skirt Row 2: turkey, shirt, bird, fir <u>Sentences:</u> 1. churn 2. turtle 3. letter 4. turkey 5. skirt 6. fir 7. bird 8. shirt

Day 4: Review the 'r' controlled blends 'ar, ir, ur, er, and or.' On a chart record the following words: purse, short, herd, bark, third, chirp, burst, tarts. Look at the words on the chart carefully and say the word that answers each clue that I say. **Clues:** 1. I am found on the outside of a tree (bark) 2. I am a case that holds someone's money. (purse) 3. It is the opposite to the word tall. (short) 4. It is a group of animals. (herd) 5. The Queen of Hearts like to make them for the king. (tarts) 6. It comes between second and fourth. (third) 8. A balloon may do this when it is blown up too big. (burst) 8. It is a sound birds make. (chirp)

Activity Worksheet: Page 119 The students are to choose the correct word to fit the sentence and print it on the line. **Answer Key:** 1. dirt 2. born 3. farm 4. porch 5. perk 6. cord 7. barn 8. tore 9. tar 10. turn

Day 5: A. Auditory Test on the 'R' Controlled Blends 'ar, or, ur, er, ir': Page 120 The students are to circle the 'r' controlled blend heard in each word given by the teacher. **Words:** 1. church 2. born 3. skirt 4. after 5. yard 6. churn 7. cork 8. girl 9. rubber 10. card 11. jar 12. stir **Answer Key:** 1. ur 2. or 3. ir 4. er 5. ar 6. ur 7. or 8. ir 9. er 10. ar 11. ar 12. ir

B. Visual Discrimination Test on the 'R' Controlled Blends 'ar, or, er, ur, ir' The students are to spell the word using an 'r' controlled blend for each picture. **Answer Key:** Row 1: bird, yarn, harp, fire Row 2: horn, stork, fur, farmer Row 3: rubber, girl, corn, shark Row 4: cork, church, fork, skirt

Name: _____ Day 1 | Week 19

 Did you know that the vowel sounds '**a, e, i, o,** and **u**' are **not** always **heard** in a word?

If the vowel is followed by the letter '**r**,' it becomes the boss and shouts out its own name.

The 'ar' vowel sound is heard at the beginning, middle or at the end of a word.

Where do you hear the '**ar**' vowel sound in the pictures?

Print the word **beginning**, **middle** or **end** on the line under each picture.

      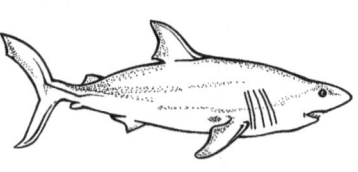

_____   _____   _____

_____   _____   _____

_____   _____   _____

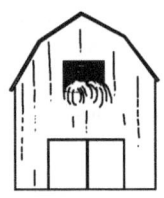      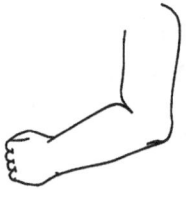

_____   _____   _____

Name: _____   Day 2 | Week 19

The letter 'r' that follows a vowel is the sound heard in some words.

Examples: car, jar, far, or, for

Print the word for each of the pictures and then **use** each word in a sentence.

_____   _____   _____   _____

_____   _____   _____   _____

1. Did you see the big _____ in the sky last night.

2. My mother made my sweater with red and white _____.

3. Put a _____ in the bottle to keep the water inside.

4. My brother and I often go to the _____ to play on the swings.

5. My dad got a new _____ for us to ride in.

6. Use your _____ to eat your dinner, not your fingers!

7. I walked along the _____ of the big lake.

8. The _____ was full of all kinds of toys.

Name: _____ Day 3 | Week 19

In some words the letter 'r' is very bossy and the vowel before it **cannot** be heard.

Examples: t<u>ur</u>tle, wat<u>er</u>, st<u>ir</u>

Use each word in the Word Box to **name** each picture and to **complete** each sentence.

Word Box

turtle   letter   skirt   bird   turkey   shirt   churn   fir

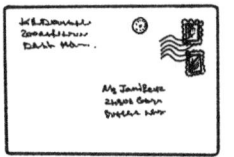   

_____ _____ _____ _____

_____ _____ _____ _____

1. Many years ago people made butter with a _____.

2. The old _____ slowly walked into the pond.

3. I sent a _____ to my grandmother and grandfather.

4. A _____ is a big bird that says gobble, gobble.

5. Mary wore her new blue _____ to school.

6. We like to buy a _____ tree at Christmas.

7. A baby _____ likes to eat all day long.

8. Mark wore a cowboy _____ with his jeans.

Name: _____   Day 4 | Week 19

In some words the letter 'r' is heard and the **vowel** ahead of it is **not** heard.

Examples: art, her, bird, fur

Sometimes the 'r' and the **vowel** join together to make **one** sound.

Examples: for, north, cord, port

Which word belongs in the sentence? **Circle it** and **print it** on the line in each sentence.

1. My father put new _____ in the flower beds. (dart, dirt)

2. I was _____ on a snowy day in January. (burn, barn, born)

3. Cows, sheep, and pigs are often seen at a _____. (firm, farm, form)

4. We sat outside on our front _____ last night. (perch, porch)

5. My dog will _____ up his ears when he hears something. (pork, park, perk)

6. I tied up the box with some _____. (card, cord)

7. A _____ is a home for farm animals. (burn, born, barn)

8. Bill _____ a hole in his pants when he climbed the fence. (tire, tore)

9. The men put some _____ on the road to fix the big crack. (turn, torn, tar)

10. You are to _____ down the next street. (turn, torn, tart)

Name: _____   Day 5 | Week 19

A. Auditory Test on the 'R' Controlled Blends 'ar, er, ir, or, and ur'

1. ur ar ir	2. ar or ir	3. ur ir ar	4. ir ur er
5. ar or ur	6. ir ar ur	7. or ir ar	8. ur ar ir
9. ar or er	10. ir or ar	11. or ar ur	12. ir er or

B. Visual Discrimination Test on the 'R' Controlled Blends 'ar, er, ir, or, ur'

Week 20: Hard and Soft 'Cc' and 'Gg'

Objective: To introduce the hard and soft sounds made by the letters **'Cc' and 'Gg'** and when they are heard in words

Day 1: Introduce the hard and soft sounds made by the letter **'Cc'**. On a chart, record the following words: cake, colour, cup. Have the students read the words aloud. Discuss the sound heard at the beginning of each word. (the letter 'Cc' makes the sound 'cuh') When the letter 'Cc' is in front of the letters 'a, o, or u it has a hard sound that says 'cuh.' Record these words on the chart: cent, city, cymbal. Say the words. What do you notice about the letter 'Cc' this time. (It makes the same sound as the letter 'Ss.') Explain that the letter 'Cc' has a hard sound and a soft sound. The hard 'Cc' says 'cuh' in front of the vowels 'a, o, and u.' Its soft sound is heard when it is in front of the vowels 'e, i, and y.'

Picture Key: Row 1: celery, carrot, cake, pencil Row 2: ice, cat, cent, cork Row 3: corn, circle, calf, mice Row 4: dancer, candle, fence, cow

Activity Worksheet: Page 122 The students are to record 'Hard C' or Soft C' on the line under each picture.
Answer Key: Row 1: soft c, hard c, hard c, soft c Row 2: soft c, hard c, soft c, hard c Row 3: hard c, soft c, hard c, soft c Row 4: soft c, hard c, soft c, hard c

Day 2: Introduce the hard and soft sounds made by the letter 'Gg.' On a chart record the following sentences. Underline the words. **Sentences:** 1. The goat, goose, and gopher gobbled up all the good plants in the garden. 2. The gentle giant brought some cabbages for the huge giraffe to eat. Read sentence #1. Discuss the underlined words. What letter does each underlined word begin with? (Gg) What sound does the 'Gg' make? (guh) Discuss sentence #2. What letter do you see again in many of the underlined words? (the letter 'Gg') Let's read the sentence together. Does the letter 'Gg' make the same sound in the underlined words as in sentence #1? (No) What sound do you hear this time? (juh) Explain that the letter 'Gg' can make two sounds. At the beginning of words, it makes the hard "Gg' sound 'guh.' Inside words it makes the soft sound that 'Jj' makes, 'juh.'

Picture Key: Row 1: game, giraffe, guitar, gift   Row 2: hinge, grass, cage, gun Row 3: angel, goat, stage, girl Row 4: gate, badge, goose, orange

Activity Worksheet: Page 123 The students are to identify the Hard 'Gg' and the Soft 'Gg' in words. **Answer Key:** Row 1: Hard G, Soft G, Hard G, Hard G Row 2: Soft G, Hard C, Soft G, Hard G Row 3: Soft G, Hard G, Soft G, Hard G Row 4: Hard G, Soft G, Hard G, Soft G

Day 3: List the following words on a chart: gas, page, goat, gym, huge, gum, stage, gull. Have the students say the words with you. They are to circle the words on the chart with the Hard 'Gg' sound and underline the words with the Soft 'Gg' sound. Record the following words on the chart: cabin, cent, carrot, face, dance, cape, cold, cell, city, cute. Have the students say the words with you. Then have them circle the words with a hard 'Cc' sound and underline the words with a soft 'Cc' sound

Picture Key: Row 1: candle, page, mice, cube Row 2: cage, camel, face, coat Row 3: game, badge, gorilla, fence Row 4: stage, cent, gum, angel

Activity Worksheet: Page 124 The students are to record the sound, Hard Gg, Soft Gg, Hard Cc, and Soft Cc on the line for each picture. **Answer Key:** Row 1: Hard C, Soft G, Soft C , Hard C Row 2: Soft G, Hard C, Soft C, Hard C Row 3: Hard G, Soft G, Hard G, Soft C Row 4: Soft Gg, Soft C, Hard G, Soft G

Day 4: Record the following words on a chart: magic, gas, candy, germs, good, cave, garden, rice, huge. Have the students classify the letters 'g' and c' as hard or soft sounds. They are to circle the hard 'Cc' and 'Gg' sounds and box the soft 'Cc' and 'Gg' sounds.

Activity Worksheet: Page 125 The students are to complete each word with a Hard or Soft 'Cc' and 'Gg.'
Answer Key: Words - 1. c 2. g 3. c 4. c 5. g 6. g 7. c 8. g 9. c 10. g 11. c 12. c **Sentences -** 1. gum 2. cage 3. stage 4. ice 5. mice 6. ice 7. game 8. goose

Day 5: A. Auditory Test on Hard and Soft 'Cc' and 'Gg': Page 126 The students are to circle the Hard or Soft 'Cc' and 'Gg' heard in each word said by the teacher. **Words:** 1. gopher 2. cell, 3. badge 4. gold 5. fancy 6. garden 7. fudge 8. comb **Answer Key:** 1. Hard G 2. Soft C 3. Soft G 4. Hard G 5. Soft C 6. Hard G 7. Soft G 8. Hard C

B. Visual Discrimination Test on the Hard and Soft 'Cc' and 'Gg': The students are to complete the spelling of each word with a Hard or Soft 'Cc' or 'Gg.' **Answer Key:** 1. c 2. g 3. g 4. c 5. g 6. g 7. c 8. g 9. c 10. c 11. g 12. g 13. g 14. c 15. g 16. g 17. c 18. g

Name: _____ Day 1 | Week 20

The letter 'Cc' may have a **hard** or a **soft** sound.

When the letter 'Cc' is in front of the vowels '**a**, **o**, or **y**,' it may have a **hard sound** that you hear for the letter '**k**.'

Examples: cake, cave, can

If the letter 'Cc' is in front of the vowel '**e**, **i**, or **y**,' it often has the **soft sound** that you hear in the letter '**Ss**.'

Examples: cent, city, lacy

Print the sound that the letter 'Cc' is making on the line under each picture.

Is it the **Hard 'c'** or the **Soft 'c?'**

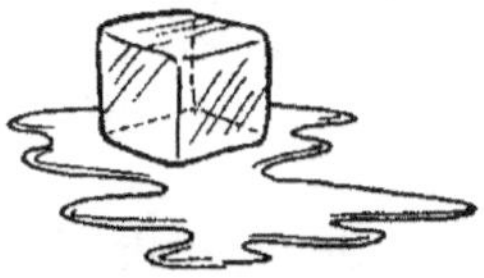

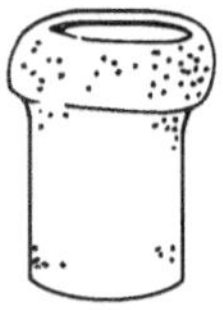

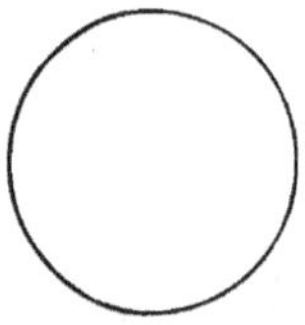

Name: _____ Day 2 | Week 20

The letter 'Gg' has **two** sounds.

It can have the **Hard 'g'** sound as in 'game, gate, and goat.'

It can have the **Soft 'g'** sound as in 'giant, magic, and cage.'

The **Hard 'g'** has the 'g' sound as in **gun** while the **Soft 'g'** has the 'j' sound as in **cage**.

Under each picture print the sound that you hear the letter 'Gg' make in each one.

Is it the Hard 'g' or the Soft 'g?'

_____ _____ _____ _____

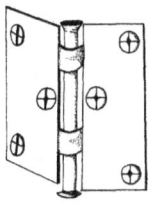  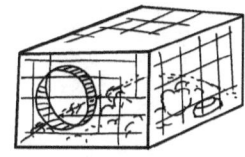 

_____ _____ _____ _____

  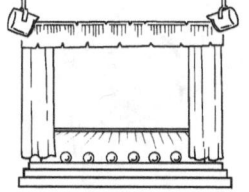 

_____ _____ _____ _____

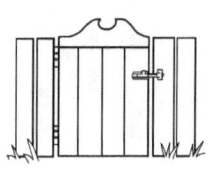   

_____ _____ _____ _____

Name: _____   Day 3 | Week 20

There are many words with the **hard** and **soft** sounds of the letters '**Cc**' and '**Gg**.'

Some of them begin with the **hard 'Cc'** or '**Gg**' or have the **soft sound** inside.

Examples: cab, cent ; gold, angel

Which sound do you hear in each picture?

Is it the **Hard Cc, Soft Cc, Hard Gg,** or **Soft Gg**?

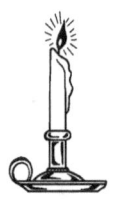   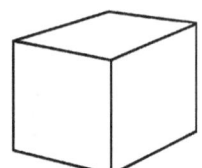

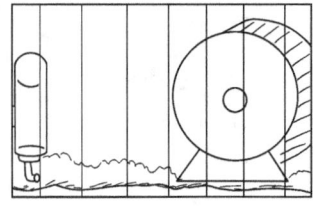   

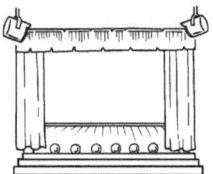   

Name: _____   Day 4 | Week 20

Hard and Soft Cc and Gg

The hard and soft '**Cc**' and '**Gg**' are often seen at the beginning, inside, or at the end of a word.

Examples: cage, giant, game, cane, dance, city

1. Print the letter '**c**' or the letter '**g**' in each group of letters to make a word.

1. spi___e   2. ___oose   3. ___one   4. dan___e

5. ___um   6. ca___e   7. ra___e   8. ___ame

9. ___orn   10. sta___e   11. i___e   12. mi___e

2. Use **some** of the words to **complete** the sentences below.

1. I like to chew bubble _____ and blow big bubbles.

2. The little bunny did not like being in a _____.

3. My class stood on the _____ and sang a funny song.

4. Will you put some _____ in my drink to make it cold.

5. The _____ looked all over the kitchen for something to eat.

6. The boy was eating a chocolate _____ cream cone.

7. I like to play a _____ called Snakes and Ladders.

8. The _____ honked loudly and chased the fox away.

Name: _____   Day 5 | Week 20

A. Auditory Test on the Sounds Made By the Hard and Soft 'Cc' and 'Gg'

1. Hard Cc Soft Cc Hard Gg Soft Gg	2. Hard Cc Soft Cc Hard Gg Soft Gg	3. Hard Cc Soft Cc Hard Gg Soft Gg	4. Hard Cc Soft Cc Hard Gg Soft Gg
5. Hard Cc Soft Cc Hard Gg Soft Gg	6. Hard Cc Soft Cc Hard Gg Soft Gg	7. Hard Cc Soft Cc Hard Gg Soft Gg	8. Hard Cc Soft Cc Hard Gg Soft Gg

B. Visual Discrimination Test on the Hard and Soft 'Cc' and 'Gg'

Is the missing letter the **Hard 'Cc'**, **Soft 'Cc'**, **Hard 'Gg'** or **Soft 'Gg?'**

1. ___ orn	7. ra ___ e	13. an ___ el
2. oran ___ e	8. hu ___ e	14. ___ ity
3. ___ ood	9. ___ ent	15. ___ ood
4. fa ___ e	10. la ___ e	16. ma ___ ic
5. ___ oat	11. ___ old	17. ___ ub
6. ___ irl	12. ___ un	18. ___ ate

Week 21: Regular Double Vowels 'ai' and 'ay'

Objective: To make students aware of the double vowel combinations **'ai'** and **'ay'**

Day 1: Introduce the double vowel combination **'ai'** with the following words recorded on a chart. **Words:** fair, rain, chair, hair Say each word after me. What do you hear inside each word? (long a) What letters are the same in each word? (ai) Explain that sometimes two vowels travel together in a word as a double vowel. Which vowel in this pair is doing all the talking? Is it the long or short 'a?' (long a) Which vowel is silent? (i)

Activity Worksheet: Page 128 The students will circle the words in the box that follow the rule. They are to spell the word that matches each meaning. **Answer Key:** 1. hair, pail, pain, chair, paint, mail, sail, tail 2. plain, stain, chair, pail, hair, jail, train, fair

Day 2: Record the following words on a chart. **Words:** say, tray, hay, day Have the students say the words. How are these words the same? (They all end with 'ay.') What sound do you hear in each one? (long a sound) The 'ay' vowel group is usually found at the end of a word and has the long 'a' sound. Listen to each of these words and tell me which vowel group you hear making the long 'a' sound. Is it 'ay' or 'ai?' How do you know? 1. play (ay, end of word) 2. pain (ai middle of word) 3. tray (ay, end of word) 4. may (ay, end of word) 5. pain (ai, middle of word) 6. hay (ay, end of word) 7. pail (ai, middle of word) 8. spray (ay, end of word)

Picture Key: Row 1: hay, lay, jay, play Row 2: tray. spray, crayons, day

Activity Worksheet: Page 129 The students will name each picture and use the words to complete the sentences. **Answer Key: A-** <u>Pictures-</u> Row 1: hay, lay, jay, play Row 2: tray, spray, crayons, day **B:** <u>Words:</u> 1. hay 2. jay 3. play 4. spray 5. day 6. crayons 7. tray 8. lay

Day 3: Review the **'ai'** and **'ay'** digraphs. Record the following words on a chart: 1. __m 2. dr__n 3. g__ 4. cl__ 5. p__n 6. st__n 7. t__l 8. tr__n 9. d__ 10. gr__n Have the students record 'ay' or 'ai' on the line to make a word. (aim, drain, gay, clay, pain, stain, tail, train, day, grain)

Picture Key: Row 1: braids, hay, snail, tray Row 2: spray, crayons, chain, pail

Activity Worksheet: Page 130 The students are to record the word for each picture and then use the words to complete the sentences. **Answer Key:** <u>Pictures</u> - Row 1: braids, hay, snail, tray Row 2: spray, crayons, chain, pail <u>Sentences:</u> 1. hay 2. snail 3. tray 4. braids 5. pail 6. spray 7. crayons 8. chain

Day 4: Record the following words on a chart: bait, stray, nail, bray, trail, waist, clay, jail. Have the students locate the word that matches each clue. **Clues:** 1. part of each finger and toe (nail) 2. a path in the woods (trail) 3. the sound that a donkey makes (bray) 4. to wander away (stray) 5. a kind of mud (clay) 6. the middle part of your body (waist) 7. a place for bad people (jail) 8. used to catch fish (bait)

Activity Worksheet: Page 131 The students are to circle words that have **'ai'** and **'ay'** double vowels. The circled words are to be printed in the sentences. **Answer Key:** <u>Words circled in Word Search are:</u> brain, rail, stay, chain, gay, clay, drain, hay, train, way **Sentences:** 1. way 2. drain 3. brain 4. gay 5. train 6. clay 7. rail

Day 5: Auditory Test on the Vowel Digraphs 'ai' and 'ay': Page 132 The students are to circle the digraph that is heard in each word said by the teacher. **Words:** 1. chain 2. play 3. paint 4. nail 5. day 6. mail 7. sway 8. train **Answer Key:** 1. ai 2. ay 3. ai 4. ai 5. ay 6. ai 7. ay 8. ai

B. Visual Discrimination Test on Words with the Vowel Digraphs 'ai' and 'ay': The students are to complete each sentence with the missing word. **Answer Key:** 1. mail 2. chain 3. stay 4. chair 5. May, play 6. stain 7. nail 8. day, rain

Name: _____ Day 1 | Week 21

Some words have two vowels together in a word that make one sound.

Examples: pair, pail, pain

The vowel 'a' does all the talking while the vowel 'i' is silent.

1. **Circle** the words in the box that follow this rule.

made	hair	cat	man	pail
cave	pain	chair	paint	band
mail	tall	sail	some	tail

2. Can you **spell** the word for each meaning?

- not pretty _____

- a bad mark on something that will not come out _____

- a place to sit _____

- it can hold water and milk _____

- it covers the top of your head _____

- a place that holds bad people _____

- it travels on tracks across the country _____

- a place to have fun on rides _____

Name: _____   Day 2 | Week 21

Other letters make the **long 'a'** sound in words.

The letters '**a**' and '**y**' make the same sound together as the letters '**a**' and '**i**' in a word.

Examples: day, pay, say, may

The letter '**a**' does all the talking and the '**y**' is silent.

Is it **ay** or **ai**?

A. **Match** the words in the Word Box to each picture.
   Print it on the line under the picture.

Word Box
crayons   jay   spray   play   hay   day   tray   lay

B. Print a picture word in each sentence.
   1. Horses like to eat lots of _____.
   2. The blue_____ is a pretty bird seen in the winter.
   3. I like to _____ with my friends in the snow.
   4. Do not _____ me with water from the hose.
   5. Every _____ I brush my teeth after I eat.
   6. I like to use my _____ to colour pictures in a book.
   7. I had to carry the drinks on a _____.
   8. A hen may _____ three eggs each day in her nest.

Name: _____   Day 3 | Week 21

The vowel digraphs 'ai' and 'ay' are often heard inside or at the end of words.

The digraph 'ai' is heard inside a word such as tail, pail and sail.' The digraph 'ay' is often heard at the end of a word such as say, day, and may.'

A. **Print** the word that names each picture on the line under each one.

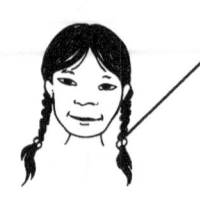   

_____   _____   _____   _____

_____   _____   _____   _____

B. **Print** a picture word in each sentence.

1. The farmer cut his _____ and put it in the barn.

2. The little _____ crawled slowly on the green leaf of the plant.

3. Carry the dirty dishes on the _____ to the kitchen.

4. The little girl had her hair in two long _____.

5. Fill the _____ with clean water.

6. We will _____ water on the car to clean it.

7. A box of _____ has eight colours.

8. The truck pulled the old car with a _____ to the dump.

Name: _____   Day 4 | Week 21

Look in the Word Search for words that have the letters 'ai' and 'ay.'

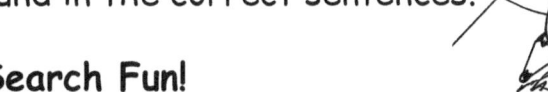

Circle each one.

Print some of the words that you found in the correct sentences.

Word Search Fun!

1. I cannot find my _____ home and I feel afraid.

2. My ring went down the _____ with the water.

3. My _____ helps me to think about my school work.

4. On my birthday I feel very happy and _____

5. The _____ flew fast along the tracks.

6. I can make things out of _____.

7. The horse jumped over the top _____ of the fence.

Name: _____   Day 5 | Week 21

A. Auditory Test on the Vowel Digraphs 'ai' and 'ay

1. ai ay	2. ai ay	3. ai ay	4. ai ay
5. ai ay	6. ai ay	7. ai ay	8. ai ay

B. Visual Discrimination Test on Words with the Vowel Digraphs 'ai' and 'ay.'

chain stay day play may nail rain chair stain mail

1. Letters get to your house in the _____.

2. The big dog broke his _____ and ran away.

3. Please _____ in the back yard with your bat and ball.

4. Sit on a _____ at the table when you eat your meals.

5. _____ I go and _____ with my friends for a while?

6. The chocolate candy left a _____ on the little girl's dress.

7. _____ a board to cover the hole in the wall.

8. All _____ long the _____ fell from the clouds

Week 22: Long 'e' Vowel Digraphs 'ee' and 'ea' and their long 'e' sound

Objective: To make students aware of the double vowel combinations 'ee' and 'ea' and their long 'e' sound.

Day 1: On a chart print the following words. **Words:** bean, leaf, seal, seat, team Have the students listen to each word and repeat it after it has been said by the teacher. What sound do you hear inside each word? (long 'e') What two letters do you see inside each word? (ea) What are the letters 'e' and 'a' called? (vowels) Which vowel is doing all the talking and can be heard? (e) Is it the long or short sound of 'e?' (the long sound) Which vowel is silent? (a) Remind the students of the saying used in previous lessons: When two vowels go walking the first one does the talking and the second one is silent.

Picture Key: Row 1: beach, beads, peas, seal Row 2: dream, eagle, leaf, beak Row 3: meat, peach, seat, beans

Activity Worksheet: Page 134 The students will match the word to each picture and print it on the line. **Answer Key:** Row 1: beach, beads, peas, seal Row 2: dream, eagle, leaf, beak Row 3: meat, peach, seat, beans

Day 2: On a chart print the following words: bee, cheek, sheep, peek, meet. Have the students listen to each word and have them repeat each one after it has been said. What sound do you hear inside each word? (the long 'e' vowel sound) What letters do you see inside each word? (ee) Which vowel is doing all the talking and is saying its own name? (the first 'e') Which vowel is not talking at all? (the second 'e') Is the first vowel the long or short 'e?' (long e) Remind the students of the saying about two vowels walking together.

Picture Key: Row 1: bee, cheek, cheese, creek Row 2: geese, heel, jeep, knee Row 3: queen, sheep, teeth, wheel

Activity Worksheet: Page 135 The students are to print the name of the picture, from the Word Box, on the line under each one. **Answer Key:** Row 1: bee, cheek, cheese, creek Row 2: geese, heel, jeep, knee Row 3: queen, sheep, teeth, wheel

Day 3: Discuss the usage of the vowel dipthongs in words. Words with the 'ee' digraph are action words. Those with the 'ea' digraph are things. On a chart record the following pairs of words: see, sea; read, reed; steal, steel; meet, meat. Discuss each pair of words. Explain that the words sound the same but have different meanings and spellings. One is an action word and one is a thing. Have the students classify the words.

Activity Worksheet: Page 136 The students are to select the correct word for each sentence and to print it on the line. **Answer Key:** 1. week 2. steel 3. meet 4. weak 5. steal 6. meat 7. creek 8. sea 9. creak 10. see

Day 4: Record on a chart the following words: creep, dream, neat, reach, weep, speech, breeze, cheap Have the students locate the words that have the following meanings. Which word on the chart means: 1. gentle wind (breeze) 2. not expensive (cheap) 3. a way to move over the floor (creep) 4. to be tidy (neat) 5. to grab something high (reach) 6. a long talk (speech) 7. to cry tears (weep) 8. pictures seen while asleep (dream)

Activity Worksheet: Page 137 The students are to locate words in the word search that have the 'ea' and 'ee' digraphs. The words are then to be used to complete the sentences. **Answer Key:** Words in the Word Search - bee, creep, leaf, teeth, beach, wheels, cheese, peach **Sentences:** 1. cheese 2. bee 3. beach 4. leaf 5. peach 6. teeth 7. wheels 8. creep

Day 5: A. Auditory Test on the Vowel Digraphs 'ea' and 'ee': The sudents are to circle the vowel digraph that is in each word said. **Words:** 1. cream 2. bee 3. cheek 4. clean 5. seal 6. jeep 7. knee 8. mean **Answer Key:** 1. ea 2. ee 3. ee 4. ea 5. ea 6. ee 7. ee 8. ea

B. Visual Discrimination Test on Words with the Vowel Digraphs 'ea' and 'ee': The student is to complete each sentence with the correct word in the Word Box. **Answer Key:** 1. dream 2. tea 3. bleed 4. knee 5. sheep 6. scream 7. green 8. beak 9. heel 10. beach

Name: _____   Day 1 | Week 22

A **digraph** is a sound made when **two** letters join together and make **one** sound.

The letters '**e**' and '**a**' make the digraph '**ea**.'

The letter '**e**' does all the talking and the '**a**' is silent.

Match the words in the box to their pictures. **Print** each picture's name on the line under it.

Words					
beach	beads	beak	beans	eagle	dream
meat	peas	seat	leaf	seal	peach

SSR1141 ISBN: 9781771586870   134   © On The Mark Press

Name: _____   Day 2 | Week 22

In some word you will find two letter 'e's walking together.

The first 'e' does all the talking and the second 'e' is silent.

Examples: feel, feed, feet

Match the words in the Word box to its picture. **Print** each one on the line under it.

Word Box					
bee	cheek	jeep	geese	wheel	cheese
heel	creek	knee	queen	sheep	teeth

 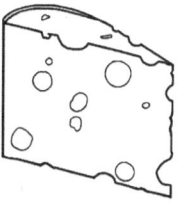 

_____   _____   _____   _____

   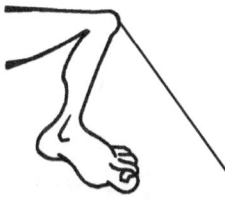

_____   _____   _____   _____

  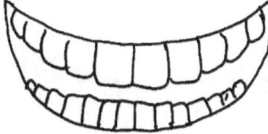 

_____   _____   _____   _____

Name: _____ Day 3 | Week 22

 Some words that have the vowel digraphs 'ea' and 'ee' look almost the same but do have different meanings.

Examples: I like to eat **meat** for supper.

I will **meet** you at the show.

The word '**meat**' is a kind of food that we eat. The word '**meet**' means to see someone.

Match the words in the Word Box to make correct sentences.

Word Box

see   sea   creak   creek   steel   steal   week   weak   meet   meat

1. I spend a _____ at my Grandmother's house every summer.

2. _____ is used to build large buildings in cities.

3. I will _____ you at the park to play ball.

4. The sick boy was too _____ to walk.

5. People should not _____ things from stores.

6. What kind of _____ are we having for supper?

7. My brother and I played in the _____ when it was hot.

8. The waves on a _____ can be very high.

9. Old rocking chairs will _____ when people sit in them.

10. I went to the circus to _____ the clowns.

Name: _____ 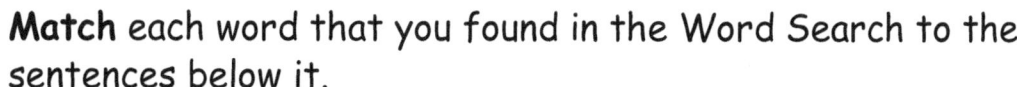 Day 4 | Week 22

Many words have the vowel digraphs 'ea' and 'ee.'

Circle the words in the Word Search that have the 'ee' and 'ea' vowel digraphs.

Match each word that you found in the Word Search to the sentences below it.

Word Search

```
m h j u i k l h j c m o p l m k n h g y s t u v w m
f g b e e h j i m r n m o p q l n m k o p g h m n v
b v f g h i v m l e n m j k l e m l b t e e t h b n
m n o k l g f d s e n m k i e n m k l p o m n b v c
b n m o p q w e b p n k l o a h y u e m o n o p q r
e c q r t y f g h b v b n m f o p l m c h e e s e m
a a n m b v c x z a s d f g h j u i o t y r s e w c
c a f g b v c h j u k l o p u y t r e w m n g v f k
h c b n w h e e l s n m o p d e r p e a c h m k l o
b v c f r t y u h j i k o l m o p y u t e r s o t y
```

Sentences:

1. Mice like to eat lots of _____.

2. The _____ flew inside a pretty flower.

3. It is fun to play in the sand at a _____.

4. The wind blew the little _____ off the tree branch.

5. A _____ is a yellow fruit that grows on a tree.

6. You should brush your _____ after you eat.

7. A car rides on four _____ on a road.

8. The baby likes to _____ on the floor.

Name: _____   Day 5 | Week 22

A. Auditory Test on the Vowel Digraphs 'ea' and 'ee.'

1. ea ee	2. ea ee	3. ea ee	4. ea ee
5. ea ee	6. ea ee	7. ea ee	8. ea ee

B. Visual Discrimination Test of the Vowel Digraphs 'ea' and 'ee'

Match each word to a sentence.

Word Box

beach	knee	beak	green	scream
sheep	heel	tea	dream	bleed

1. You may do this at night when you sleep. _____

2. I am a hot drink. _____

3. This happens when you cut yourself. _____

4. I am a part of your leg. _____

5. We are white and black farm animals with wool coats. _____

6. You may do this when you are afraid. _____

7. I am the colour of grass. _____

8. It is part of a bird's body. _____

9. I am part of your foot. _____

10. You can swim and play here. _____

Week 23: Long 'i' Digraphs 'igh' and 'ie'

Objective: To make students aware that the **long 'i'** sound can be spelled **'ie'** or **'igh.'**

Day 1: On a chart record the following words: kite, hive, fire. Say and discuss the words. What vowel sound do you hear in each word? (long i) Explain that there are other words that have the long 'i' sound. Sometimes more than one letter makes the sound. Print the following words on the chart: high, night, fight. Say the words and underline the 'igh' in each word. Record the words 'lie, tries, fries' on the chart. Say the words and underline the 'ie' sound. Explain to your students that the vowel **'i'**, the letters **'ie'** and **'igh'** all make the **long 'i' vowel** sound in words.

Picture Key: Row 1: fight, tie, high, fries Row 2: cries, pie, night, bright Row 4: lie, fright, check mark for right, thigh

Activity Worksheet: Page 140 The students are to complete each word under the picture with the correct sound. **Answer Key:** Row 1: igh, ie, igh, ie Row 2: ie, ie, igh, igh Row 3: ie, igh, igh, igh

Day 2: Review the **long 'i'** sound made by **'i, igh**, and **ie.'** Record the sounds at the top of a chart. Review what they say and where you might see them. Dictate words for the students to spell on the chart.
Words: lie, high, pie, right, bike, lies, night, kite. Have the students underline the long 'i' sound in each word.

Activity Worksheet: Page 141 The students are to match the words to their meanings and record them on the lines. **Answer Key:** 1. light 2. night 3. lies 4. tie 5. fried 6. cries 7. fight 8. right 9. sight 10. thigh

Day 3: Record the following words on a chart: flight, sigh, tight, lies, tried, spies, right, might light. Review the vowel sounds long **'i, igh**, and **ie.'** Have the students use their word attack skills to find the words on the chart that have the following meanings: 1. something you may do when you are tired or upset (sigh) 2. a trip on a plane (flight) 3. the opposite to loose (tight) 4. to secretly watch someone (spies) 5. to not tell the truth (lies) 6. opposite to left (right) 7. used to make a dark place bright (light) 8. maybe (might)

Activity Worksheet: Page 142 The students are to record the sentence beginning and complete it with a good reason. **Answer Key:** Answers will vary but sentences should be completed with a good reason.

Day 4: Record the following incomplete words on a chart. Have the students complete each word with 'igh' or 'ie.' Words: d___d (died), dr___s (dries) t___t (tight) t___ (tie), tr___s (tries) h___ (high) t___s (ties) f___t (fight). Have the students say each word.

Activity Worksheet: Page 143 The students are to complete each riddle with the correct answer. **Answer Key:** 1. thigh 2. night 3. pie 4. tie 5. fries 6. lies 7. sigh 8. fight

Day 5: A. Auditory Test on the Long 'i' Digraphs 'igh' and 'ie': Page 144
The student is to circle the long 'i' digraph that is heard in each word said by the teacher. **Words:** 1. dies 2. bright 3. lied 4. fright 5. spies 6. high 7. fight 8. tries **Answer Key:** 1. ie 2. igh 3. ie 4. igh 5. ie 6. igh 7. igh 8. ie

B. Visual Discrimination Test on Words with the Long i' Digraphs 'igh' and 'ie'
The students are to match each word to a sentence. **Answer Key:** 1. lied 2. cries 3. fried 4. night 5. tie 6. light 7. flight 8. die 9. dries 10. high

SSR1141 ISBN: 9781771586870

Name: _____   Day 1 | Week 23

"Is it 'igh' 'ie' or 'i'?"

Did you know that the **long 'i'** sound can be seen and heard **three** different ways?

Examples: l**igh**t, tr**ie**d, f**i**re

It can be seen and heard as '**igh**', '**ie**', and '**i**.'

Is the long vowel 'i' sound being made by the letters 'i', 'ie' or 'igh' in the pictures?

Print the sound on the line under each picture to complete each word.

f ___ t    t 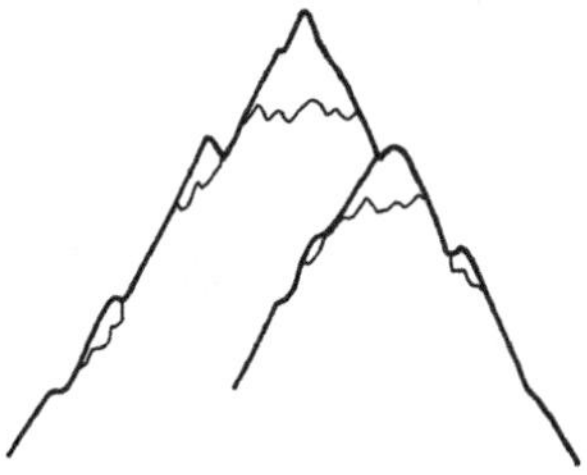 ___   h 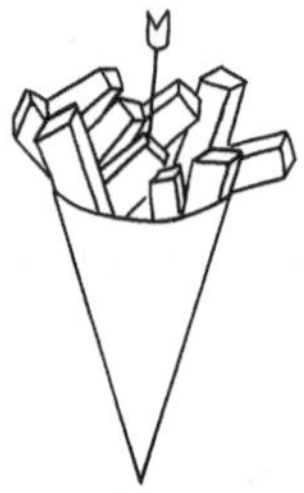 ___   fr ___ s

cr ___ s    p  ___   n ___ t    br ___ t

l  ___   fr ___ t    r ___ t 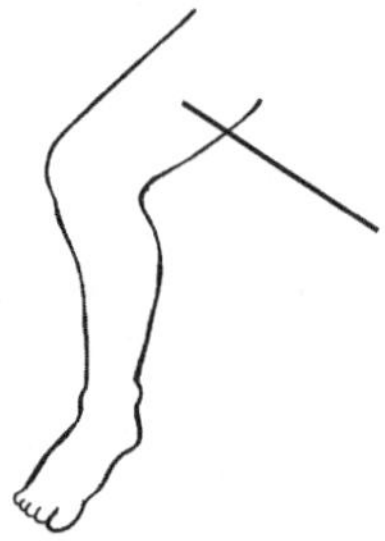   th ___

140

Name: _____ Day 2 | Week 23

Don't forget that the **long 'i'** sound can be made in three ways.

Remember it can be **alone** as in the word 'f**i**re' or it may be found in a **group of letters** such as in 'n**igh**t' and 'l**ie**d.'

Can you **match** the words in the Word Box to their meanings? **Record** each word on the line at the end of each meaning.

Word Box				
light	fried	tie	night	lies
thigh	sight	cries	right	fight

Meanings:

1. used in the dark to see _____

2. a time for resting _____

3. to tell bad things about someone or something _____

4. something a man wears around his neck _____

5. a way some potatoes are cooked _____

6. an unhappy sound made by a baby _____

7. to hit each other when angry _____

8. not wrong _____

9. someone who is blind does not have this _____

10. the top part of your leg _____

Name: _____   Day 3 | Week 23

Is it 'igh' 'ie' or 'i ?'

What do you do when you come to a word that has the vowel 'i', 'igh' or 'i?'

Of course you know that they all make the '**long i**' vowel sound.

Read the beginning of each sentence and **finish it** telling why each event may have happened.

1. Boys and girls should not fight because _____
   _____.

2. Do not climb up high in a tree because _____
   _____.

3. Telling lies is a very bad thing to do because _____
   _____.

4. The girl stood and cried because _____
   _____.

5. The dog tried to run away because _____
   _____.

6. I like eating fries because _____
   _____.

7. A door to a house should be locked at night because _____
   _____.

8. A day may be bright and warm because _____
   _____.

Name: _____   Day 4 | Week 23

Do you remember the sound made by 'igh, ie, and i?'
It is the 'long i' vowel sound.
The answer to each riddle below is a word with the
long 'i' sound. The word may have the letter 'i' or the letters
'igh' or 'ie.' Print a word from the Word Box on the line to
answer each one.

Is it 'igh' 'ie' or 'i ?'

Word Box
fight   thigh   sigh   night   pie   fries   lies   tie

1. I am part of your body. I am the top part of your leg. I am called your _____.

2. I am part of a day. It is dark outside. I am called _____.

3. Sometimes apples are put inside some dough. Then they are baked in the oven. It is called a _____.

4. I am long. I am put around your neck. Men wear me with a shirt. I am called a _____

5. Potatoes are used to make us. We are cut into sticks and cooked. We are called _____.

6. We are bad things to say. We can get you into trouble if you tell them. We are called _____.

7. I am a soft sound. You may do this if you are tired or upset. You may _____.

8. Children should not do this. Someone could get hurt. Children should not _____.

Name: _____   Day 5 | Week 23

A. Auditory Test on the Long 'i' Digraphs 'igh and 'ie'

1. igh ie	2. igh ie	3. igh ie	4. igh ie
5. igh ie	6. igh ie	7. igh ie	8. igh ie

B. Visual Discrimination Test of the Long 'i' Digraphs 'igh' and 'ie'

Match each word to a sentence. Use the words in the Word Box.

Word Box
die   light   dries   flight   tie   night   fried   cries   lied   high

1. The boy said something that was not true. _____

2. It is an unhappy sound. _____

3. The way meat may be cooked. _____

4. It is a very dark time outside your house. _____

5. It is something you do to shoelaces. _____

6. You do this to make candles glow. _____

7. It is the trip that birds make when they fly south. _____

8. In the fall, plants in gardens do this. _____

9. A dryer does this to clothes after they have been washed. _____

10. Some buildings are made big and tall. _____

Week 24: Vowel Digraphs 'oa, oe, ow, ue, ew'

Objective: To make students aware that the long 'o' vowel sound may be spelled 'oa', 'oe' and 'ow' and the long 'u' vowel sound may be spelled 'ue' and 'ew.'

Day 1: On a chart, record the following groups of words. **Group 1:** soap, road, coat **Group 2:** Joe, toe, hoe **Group 3:** crow, row, bow Have the students read the words in Group 1. What sound do you hear in each word? (long 'o') Which two letters are making the sound? ('o' and 'a') Which letter is doing all the talking? (o) Is it the long or short 'o'? (long) Do you remember the saying that you were taught earlier about two vowels together in a word? (When two vowels go walking together in a word, the first one does all the talking and says its own name.) The first vowel is usually the long vowel sound. Read the words in Group 2. What sound do you hear in this group of words? (long o) Which letters are making the sound? (oe) Read the words in Group 3. What sound do you hear in each word? (long o) Which letters are making the sound? (ow) Where are the letters found? (at the end of a word) Have the students note that 'oa' is found in the middle of a word and 'oe' and 'ow' are usually found at the end of a word.

Picture Key: Row 1: boat, crow, hoe, snow Row 2: goat, coat, soap, toad Row 3: toe, loaf, road, bow

Activity Worksheet: Page 146 The student is to match each word to its picture and print it on the line under each one. **Answer Key:** Row 1: boat, crow, hoe, snow Row 2: goat, coat, soap, toad Row 3: toe, loaf, road, bow

Day 2: Record the vowel digraphs 'oa, oe and ow' on a chart. Under each sound have a student record the spelling of each of the following words. Say: Who can spell the word: coat, crow, hoe, toad, mow, Joe, blow, doe, soap.

Picture Key: Row 1: coat, bow, toe, soap Row 2: bowl, doe, road, blow

Activity Worksheet: Page 147 The students are to record the correct spelling of the words to match the pictures. The words in the Word Box are to be used to complete the sentences. **Answers:** Pictures - Row 1: coat, bow, toe, soap Row 2: bowl, doe, road, blow Sentences: 1. toes 2. float 3. cloak 4. hoe 5. throw 6. Joe 7. goal 8. mow

Day 3: Record these words on a chart: glue, blue, flue. What letters are the same in each word? (ue) Say the words. What sound does 'ue' make in these words? (long u) Record the following words on the same chart: new, flew, grew. Which letters are the same in each word? (ew) What sound do they make. (long u) The letters oa, oe, and ou say the long 'o' sound. The letters 'ue' and 'ew' make the long 'u' sound. Which vowel digraph do you hear in each word that I say. **Words:** toe (oe); blue (ue); grew (ew); snow (ow); goat (oa); flew (ew); glue (ue); chew (ew)

Picture Key: Row 1: sky, flew, new, clue Row 2: flue, blew, stew, glue

Activity Worksheet: Page 148 The students will record the name of each picture on the line under it and then use the words to complete the sentences. **Answer Key:** Pictures - Row 1: blue, flew, new, clue Row 2: flue, blew, stew, glue Sentences: 1. glue 2. new 3. flue 4. clue 5. stew 6. blue 7. blew 8. flew

Day 4: Review the vowel digraphs: oa, oe, ow, ue, and ew with the following words. Record the words on a chart: road, toes, show, mew, clue, bow, chew, true, hoe, coach. Have the students locate the word that matches each clue. **Clues:** 1. the person who teaches a team (coach) 2. a place to see a movie (show) 3. something found to help solve a mystery (clue) 4. used to shoot an arrow (bow) 5. your teeth do this (chew) 6. the opposite to false (true) 7. the sound a kitten makes (mew) 8. a tool used in a garden (hoe) 9. something cars travel on (road) 10. There are ten of them on your feet. (toes)

Picture Key: Row 1: toe, bowl, blew, loaf Row 2: goat, glue, boat, crow

Activity Worksheet: Page 149 The students are to print the missing word for each picture and sentence found in the Word Box. **Answer Key:** Pictures - Row 1: toe, bowl, blew, loaf Row 2: goat, glue, boat, crow **Sentences:** 1. toe 2. loaf 3. blew 4. bowl 5. glue 6. crow 7. boat 8. goat

Day 5: A. Auditory Test on the Vowel Digraphs 'oa, oe, ow, ue, and ew': Page 150 The students are to circle the word spoken by the teacher in each group. **Words:** 1. bone 2. clue 3. soap 4. glow 5. blew 6. road 7. coast 8. toast

B. Visual Discrimination Test on Words with the Vowel Digraphs 'oa, oe, ow, ue, and ew': The students are to complete each sentence with a word from the Word Box. **Answer Key:** 1. load 2. float 3. true 4. flew 5. throw 6. doe 7. toad 8. glow

Name: _____   Day 1 | Week 24

 Did you know that the **long 'o'** vowel sound may be seen as '**oa**, **oe**, and **ow**' in words?

Examples: boat, toe, bow

Match the words in the Word Box to their pictures.

Print each word on the line under its picture.

Word Box					
bow	road	loaf	soap	toad	toe
coat	goat	snow	hoe	crow	boat

Name: _____ Day 2 | Week 24

Don't forget the sounds that the **long 'o' vowel** can make with the letters **'a, e,** and **w.'**

Examples: goat, Joe, snow

A. How well can you **spell** the words for the pictures. **Print** the word under each one on the line

B. Print the words in the Word Box in the sentences.

Word Box

| mow | toes | float | hoe | goal | Joe | throw | cloak |

1. Sally likes to paint the nails on her _____.
2. The boat's rope broke and it began to _____ away from the dock.
3. The witch wore a black _____ when she flew on her broom.
4. Bill will use the _____ to dig up weeds in the garden.
5. How far can you _____ a ball?
6. _____ is the name of the boy that I met at school.
7. Have you ever scored a _____ during a hockey game?
8. I will _____ the lawn after school today.

Name: _____ | Day 3 | Week 24

The vowel digraphs 'ue' and 'ew' make the long 'u' sound in words.

Examples: true, clue ; new, chew

Use the words in the **Word Box** to **name** each picture and to **complete** the sentences.

Word Box
blue   flew   new   clue   flue   blew   stew   glue

1. We used _____, paper and some bags to make our puppets.
2. When can I wear my _____ dress to school?
3. Jack was sick with the _____ and could not go to school.
4. The boy looked through a glass to find a _____ about the thief.
5. Mom made a _____ with meat and vegetables for supper.
6. The fluffy white clouds floated in the _____ sky
7. I _____ a big bubble with my gum.
8. The bird _____ up to its nest with some worms.

Name: _____   Day 4 | Week 24

The vowel digraphs '**oa, oe, ow, ue,** and **ew**' are often heard in words.

Examples: oak, Joe, snow, glue, new

Use the words in the Word Box to name each picture and to complete each sentence.

Word Box
toe   bowl   blue   loaf   goat   glue   boat   crow

         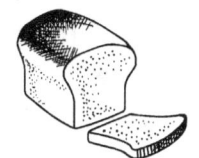

_____   _____   _____   _____

_____   _____   _____   _____

1. The boy broke his _____ when he tripped over a rock.

2. I went to the store to buy a _____ of bread.

3. The wind _____ the leaves all over the ground.

4. Put some soup in a _____ for your lunch.

5. Can I use some _____ to fix my toy car?

6. The big black _____ sat on the post to look around.

7. We went for a ride in a big _____ on the lake.

8. The little white _____ stood on the top of the pile of hay.

Name: _____ Day 5 | Week 24

A. Auditory Test one the Vowel Digraphs 'oa, oe, ow, ue, ew

1. home	2. crow	3. soap	4. goat
bone	coat	hoe	glow
toe	clue	show	glue
5. blew	6. row	7. coat	8. toast
blow	road	coast	throw
boat	rose	cone	true

B. Visual Discrimination Test on the Words with Vowel Digraphs 'oa, oe ow, ue, ew'

Word Box

glow   doe   toad   throw   true   flew   float   load

1. I helped my dad _____ his truck with wood that he had cut.

2. A boat can _____ on top of the water.

3. The story that he told was not _____.

4. The player hit the ball and it _____ over the fence.

5. How far can you _____ a baseball?

6. A mother deer is called a _____.

7. The little _____ hopped under a bush to hide from the big bird.

8. The lights on the Christmas tree _____ at night in the dark.

Week 25: Review of the Vowel Digraphs 'ai, ay, ee, ea, ie, igh, oa, ow, ew, ue'

Objective: To reinforce the recall and usage of the long vowel digraphs in students' word attack skills.

Day 1: Review the vowel digraphs 'ai, ay, ea, ee.' On a chart record the following unfinished words: 1. pl ___ 2. j___l 3. t ___ 4. f___d 5. tr ___ 6. m ___ l 7. h ___ l 8. s ___ l Have the students complete each word with one of the vowel digraphs 'ay, ai, ee, ea.' **Possible Words:** 1. play 2. jail 3. tea 4. feed 5. tray or tree 6. mail or meal 7. hail or heel 8. sail or seal

Picture Key: Row 1: hay, rain, jeep, ear Row 2: seeds, play, dream, chain

Activity Worksheet: Page 152 The students will spell and record the name of each picture on the line. They are also to record the words from the Word Box that belongs in each sentence on the lines.

Picture Key: Row 1: hay, rain, jeep, ear Row 2: seeds, play, dream, chain

Answer Key: Pictures: hay, rain, jeep, ear Row 2: seeds, play, dream, chain   **Sentences -** 1. feed, hay 2. keep, jeep 3. may, play 4. hear, scream 5. rain, day 6. shear, sheep 7. steal, jail 8. pail, beets

Day 2: Review the vowel digraphs 'ie, igh, and oa.' Record them on a chart in three columns. Say one of the following words and have a student print it under the digraph heard inside it. Words: 1. tie (ie) 2. high (igh) 3. soak (oa) 4. toast (oa) 5. road (oa) 6. right (igh) 7. die (ie) 8. coach (oa) 9. toad (oa) 10. light (igh)

Picture Key: Row 1: coat, crow, soap, light Row 2: bowl, loaf, night, road

Activity Worksheet: Page 153 The students are to spell and record the name of each picture on the line.
Answer Key: Pictures Row 1: coat, crow, soap, light Row 2: bowl, loaf, night, road Sentences: 1. loaf 2. soap 3. crow 4. bowl 5. night 6. road 7. light 8. coat

Day 3: Review the '**ow**, **ew**, and **ue**' vowel digraphs. Record them on a chart. Discuss where each digraph is usually seen. '**Ow**' and '**er**' are usually seen at the ends of words. The vowel digraph '**ue**' may be seen inside or at the end of words. Record the following incomplete words on a chart and have the students complete each one with the vowel digraphs 'ow, ew, or ue' Words: yell<u>ow</u>, ch<u>ew</u>, bl<u>ow</u>, thr<u>ew</u>, tr<u>ue</u> cr<u>ow</u>, fl<u>ew</u>, sh<u>ow</u> cr<u>ue</u>l, thr<u>ow</u>,

Picture Key: Row 1: snow, glue, blew, bow Row 2: crow, stew, bowl, clue

Activity Worksheet: Page 154 The students are to spell the word for each picture and to print it on the line. The words are to be used in the sentences. **Picture Words:** 1. snow, glue, blew, bow Row 2: crow, stew, bowl, clue **Sentence Words:** 1. clue 2. bow 3. bowl 4. blew 5. glue 6. snow 7. crow 8. stew

Day 4: Review all the vowel digraphs. Record the following words on a chart. **Words:** 1. follow 2. cruel 3. dew 4. roast 5. Joe 6. right 7. tree 8. clean 9. trail 10. fight Explain to your students that you are going to give them a clue about one of the words and they are to sound out the words and find the one that matches it. **Clues:** 1. to walk after someone (follow) 2. someone who is very mean (cruel) 3. It makes the grass wet in the morning (dew) 4. a way to cook meat (roast) 5. the name of a man (Joe) 6. the opposite to left (right) 7. a very tall plant (tree) 8. the opposite to dirty (clean) 9. a kind of path (trail) 10. to hit each other (fight)

Activity Worksheet: Page 155 The students are to complete each sentence with the correct word.
Answer Key: 1. true 2. drew 3. blow 4. fairy 5. team 6. fries 7. coach 8. spray 9. right 10. hockey

Day 5: A. Auditory Test on the Vowel Digraphs 'ai, ay, ee, ea, ie, igh, oa, ow, ew, ue': Page 156 The students are to circle the vowel digraph that is heard in each word said by the teacher. **Words:** 1. fight 2. glue 3. pray 4. boat 5. team 6. show 7. tree 8. tie 9. true 10. rain **Answer Key:** 1. igh 2. ue 3. ay 4. oa 5. ea 6. ow 7. ee 8. ie 9. ue 10. ai

Visual Discrimination Test on the Vowel Digraphs 'ai, ay, ee, ea, ie, igh, oa, ow, ew, ue': The students are to chose and record the correct word for each sentence on the line provided. **Answer Key:** 1. bait 2. high 3. stay 4. cries 5. night 6. know 7. flue 8. throw 9. flew 10. treat

Name: _____ Day 1 | Week 25

Do you remember what the vowel digraphs '**ay, ai, ea,** and **ee**' say?

They are found in the words '**play, rain, meat** and **feet**.'

The vowel digraphs '**ay**' and '**ai**' make the long '**a**' sound.

The vowel digraphs '**ea**' and '**ee**' make the long '**e**' sound.

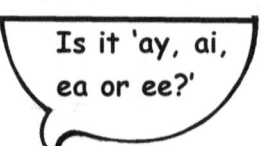
Is it 'ay, ai, ea or ee?'

A. Print the name of each picture on the line under it.

B. Use the words in the box to complete each sentence.

| feed | keep | may | hear | rain | shear | sheep | steal |
| pail | hay | jeep | play | today | scream | beets | jail |

1. Did you _____ the horse some _____?

2. Where does your father _____ his _____?

3. _____ I go to the park to _____ on the swings.

4. Did you _____ the boy _____ when he saw the bear?

5. It is going to _____ all _____ and we cannot play outside.

6. In the spring the farmer will _____ the wool from his _____.

7. People who _____ will go to _____.

8. The _____ is full of big, red _____.

SSR1141 ISBN: 9781771586870   © On The Mark Press

Name: _____   Day 2 | Week 25

Here are some more vowel digraphs for you to remember. They are '**ie, igh**, and **oa**.'

They are found in the words '**pie, high**, and **goat**.'

The vowel digraphs '**ie**' and '**igh**' make the long '**i**' sound and the vowel digraph '**oa**' makes the long '**o**' sound.

A. Print the name of each picture on the line under it.

B. Use the picture words to complete each sentence.

1. I went to the store to buy a _____ of bread.

2. Please use _____ and water to wash your hands before you eat.

3. A _____ likes to pick up shiny things and then hides them.

4. My mother put some hot porridge in a _____ for my breakfast.

5. At _____ I like to look out my bedroom window at the stars.

6. The _____ to the farm was muddy and bumpy.

7. Turn off your _____ and go to sleep.

8. It's raining outside so put on your rain_____.

Name: _____ Day 3 | Week 25

The vowel digraphs 'ow' ot 'ew' are seen most of the time at the **end** of a word.

Examples: snow, blow; blew, flew

The vowel digraph 'ue' is found **inside** words and at the **end** of words.

Examples: true, clue; duel, fuel

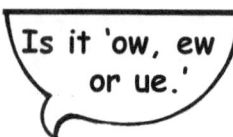

A. Print the name of each picture on the line under it.

B. Complete each sentence with a picture word.

1. The man looked for a _____ with his big magnifying glass.

2. The present was wrapped in gold paper and tied with a big red _____.

3. The soup in my _____ was very hot.

4. Who _____ the biggest bubble with their gum?

5. Use some _____ and a patch to fix the hole in your football.

6. I watched the _____ falling all over the ground.

7. The _____ is a big black bird that likes to caw.

8. My mother used some meat and vegetables to make a _____

Name: _____ Day 4 | Week 25

How good is your memory?

How well do you remember the sounds that these **vowel digraphs** make?

Where would you find them in a word?

ai, ay, ee, ea, ie, igh, oa, ow, ew, ue

Print a word from the Word Box that belongs in each sentence.

Word Box

hockey   true   right   drew   spray   blow   coach   fairy   fries   team

1. A fairy tale is not a _____ story.

2. The children _____ pictures of animals that live in Canada.

3. How many big bubbles can you _____ with your gum?

4. The _____ waved her magic wand and made all the flowers turn pink.

5. My _____ won all of the hockey games last year.

6. I like to eat _____ with my hotdog.

7. My father is the _____ of my baseball team.

8. Elephants like to _____ water at each other with their trunks.

9. I use my _____ hand for printing and drawing pictures.

10. I will meet you at the _____ rink at noon.

Name: _____   Day 5 | Week 25

A. Auditory Test on the Vowel Digraphs 'ai, ay, ee, ea, ie, igh, oa, ow, ew, ue'

1. ie igh	2. ew ue	3. ai ay	4. oa ow	5. ee ea
6. oo ow	7. ee ea	8. ie igh	9. ew ue	10. ai ay

B. Visual Discrimination Test on the Vowel Digraphs: ai, ay, ee, ea, ie, igh, oa, ow, ew, ue'

1. Worms are used for _____ to catch fish. (bay, bait, bee)

2. How _____ can your horse jump? (hail hope, high)

3. You can _____ at my house and we can play games. (hay, stay, bay)

4. My baby sister _____ all the time. (cry, cries, crying)

5. At _____, raccoons walk around looking for food. (nail, night, new)

6. Do you _____ how to find your way home. (know, knew, new)

7. The little girl is sick with the _____ and must stay home. (flew, due, flue)

8. How far can you _____ a baseball? (threw, throw, throat)

9. We _____ on a big plane to Calgary. (flue, flew, fly)

10. What is your favourite _____? (train, treat, tray)

Week 26: Diphthongs 'ou, ow, oi, oy'

Objective: To make students aware of the sounds that the vowel diphthongs '**ou**, **ow**, **oi**, and **oy**' make in words and at the end of words.

Day 1: Record the words 'mouse, house, shout, cloud on a chart. Say each word and have the students repeat it. Underline the 'ou' sound in each word. What sound do these two letters make in each word? (same sound as 'ow') It is the sound you make if someone pinches or hurts you. Where would you find the letters 'ou' in a word? (on the inside, middle) Record the words 'cow, bow, now, down' on the chart. Say each word and have the students repeat them. What two letters are the same in each word? (ow) What sound do they make? (The same sound as 'ou') What did you learn about the 'ou' and 'ow' diphthong today? (They make the same sound inside and at the end of words.) Which sound is usually found inside a word? (ou) Which sound may be inside or at the end of a word? (ow)

Picture Key: Row 1: clown, mouse, couch, howl Row 2: mouth, owl, blouse, crown Row 3: cow, towel, cloud, house

Activity Worksheet: Page 158 The students are to record the word on the line under each picture. They are to underline the diphthongs 'ou' and 'oy' in the words. **Answer Key:** Row 1: clown, mouse, couch, howl Row 2: mouth, owl, blouse, crown Row 3: cow, towel, cloud, house

Day 2: Record the following words on a chart. **Words:** boy, toy, joy, boil, oil, coil Say the words for the students. Have the students say the words. What sound do you hear in all the words? (long o) Which letters in the words are making the long 'o' sound? (oi and oy) Where is the 'oi' sound found? (inside the word) Where is the 'oy' sound found? (at the end of a word.)

Picture Key: Row 1: boy, decoy, toys, coin Row 2: point, oil, cowboy, voice Row 3: join, boil, joint, soil

Activity Worksheet: Page 159 The students will record the name of each picture on the line and circle the vowel digraph heard in each one. **Answer Key:** Row 1: b**oy**, dec**oy**, t**oy**, c**oin** Row 2: p**oin**t, **oi**l, cowb**oy**, v**oi**ce Row 3: j**oin**, b**oi**l, j**oin**t, s**oi**l

Day 3: Review the vowel dipthongs 'ou , ow, oi, and oy.' On a chart record the following incomplete words: c___n, t___, c___ch, p__nt, b__, m__se, sp__t, c__h__se, h__nd, fr__n Have the students complete each word with one of the vowel dipthongs: oy, oi, ou, ow. Review the positions where dipthongs are found in words.

Picture Key: Row 1: clown, mouth, coin, toys Row 2: cowboy, crown, point, mouse

Activity Worksheet: Page 160 The students are to record each word under its picture and then use the words to complete the sentences. **Answer Key:** <u>Pictures</u> - Row 1: clown, mouth, coin, toys, Row 2: cowboy, crown, point, mouse <u>Sentences</u> - 1. clown 2. cowboy 3. crown 4. mouse 5. mouth 6. coin 7. point 8. toy

Day 4: Review the vowel dipthongs 'oy, oi, ou, and ow. Record the following words on a chart. **Words:** 1. shout 2. noise 3 crowd 4. grouch 5. join 6. crew 7. soil 8. flew Use the following clues and have a students give a word to match each one. **Clues:** 1. to have travelled by plane (flew) 2. a grumpy person (grouch) 3. a group of people (crowd) 4. another word for dirt (soil) 5. a loud sound (noise) 6. to belong to a group (join) 6. a group of people who work together (crew) 8. to call loudly (shout)

Activity Worksheet: Page 161 The students will complete each sentence with the correct word from the Word Box. **Answer Key:** 1. boil 2. clouds 3. crowd 4. cowboy 5. howl 6. pound 7. join 8. south 9. round 10. flower

Day 5: A. Auditory Test on the Vowel Dipthongs 'ou, ow, oi, oy Page 162 The students are to circle the letters that are making the vowel sound in each word said by the teacher. **Words:** 1. plow 2. voice 3. mouth 4. town 5. couch 6. toy 7. coin 8. joy **Answer Key:** 1. ow 2. oi 3. ou 4. ow 5. ou 6. oy 7. oi 8. oy

B. Visual Discrimination Test on the Words with the Vowel Dipthongs 'ou, ow, oi, oy'
The students are to complete each sentence with a word from the Word Box. **Answer Key:** 1. toy 2. owl 3. flour 4. point 5. mouse 6. plow 7. noise 8. brown 9. cloud 10. town

SSR1141 ISBN: 9781771586870

Name: _____ Day 1 | Week 26

In some words you can hear the sound made by the letters '**ou**.'

Examples: mouse, house, shout

In other words you can hear the same sound made by '**ow**.'

Examples: bow, now, cow

Is it 'ou' or 'ow'?

The letters '**ou**' and '**ow**' make the same sound. It is the sound that you make when you hurt yourself.

The sound '**ou**' is heard **inside** a word while the sound '**ow**' may be found **inside** a word or at the **end** of it.

Record the word that matches each picture on the line. **Underline** the '**ou**' or '**ow**' sound in each word.

Word Box					
howl	couch	house	owl	cloud	cow
blouse	crown	towel	mouse	mouth	clown

Name: _____ Day 2 | Week 26

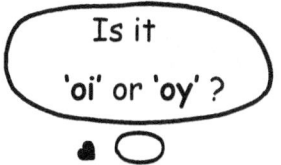
Is it 'oi' or 'oy' ?

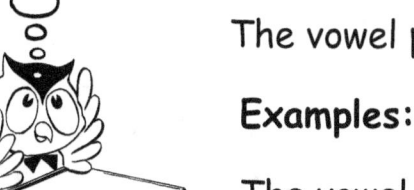

The vowel pairs '**oi**' and '**oy**' make the **long** 'o' sound in some words.

The vowel pair '**oi**' is often seen inside a word.

Examples: boil, coin, join

The vowel pair '**oy**' is often found at the end of a word.

Examples: boy, toy, joy

Record each picture's name on the line. Circle the vowel sound that you hear in each one.

Word Box

boy   coin   toys   point   decoy   oil   cowboy   voice   joint   join   soil   boil

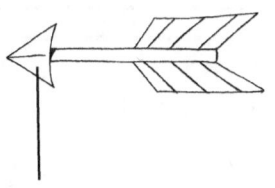   

  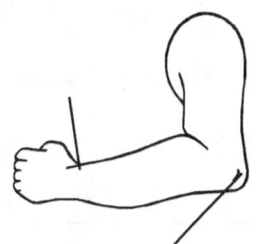 

Name: _____   Day 3 | Week 26

Which **vowel pair** is doing the talking inside or at the end of a word?

Is it '**oi, oy, ou,** or **ow?**'

Use the words in the Word Box to **name** each picture aand to **complete** each sentence.

Word Box

| mouse | point | crown | cowboy |
| toys | coin | mouth | clown |

_____ _____ _____ _____

_____ _____ _____ _____

1. The _____ liked to throw things into the air and catch them.
2. The _____ rode on a horse that jumped up and down.
3. A _____ may be worn by a king or a queen.
4. The little _____ ran quickly when it saw the cat.
5. Your tongue and teeth are found inside your _____.
6. The little boy held a silver _____ that had a deer on it.
7. It is not polite to _____ a finger at someone.
8. Which _____ would you like to play with today?

Name: _____   Day 4 | Week 26

How well can you use '**oi**, **oy**, **ou**, and **ow**' to sound out words.

Record the correct word from the Word Box to **complete** each sentence.

Use 'oi, oy, ou, and ow' to sound out your words.

Word Box

| flower | south | join | clouds | howl |
| round | boil | cowboy | crowd | pound |

1. You can _____ the potatoes in this pot.

2. The dark _____ in the sky told us it was going to rain.

3. The _____ at the hockey game cheered loudly for their teams.

4. I saw a _____ rope a little calf at the fair.

5. I heard the wolf _____ loudly late at night.

6. Did you hear someone _____ on our door during the night?

7. Do you think the boys will let a girl _____ their secret club?

8. Jason watched the birds fly _____ in October.

9. A ball has a _____ shape and can bounce.

10. The yellow _____ in the garden is called a daffodil.

Name: _____   Day 5 | Week 26

A. Auditory Test on the Vowel Dipthongs 'ou, ow, oi, oy'

1. oi oy	2. oi oy	3. oi oy	4. oi oy
ou ow	ou ow	ou ow	ou ow
5. oi oy	6. oi oy	7. oi oy	8. oi oy
ou ow	ou ow	ou ow	ou ow

B. Visual Discrimination Test on Words with the Vowel Dipthongs 'ou, ow, oi, oy'

Word Box

owl   point   plow   brown   noise   mouse   flour   toy   cloud   town

1. I gave my little brother a _____ truck for Christmas.

2. The big _____ sat in a tree and watched for an animal to eat.

3. We used an egg, _____ and milk to make our pancakes.

4. "Do not _____ your finger at me!" cried the angry boy.

5. The little grey _____ ran away quickly when it saw the big cat.

6. In the spring, farmers _____ their fields and plant crops.

7. What is making that _____ outside the house?

8. I have a new _____ coat to wear in the winter.

9. A dark _____ in the sky told us it was going to rain.

10. I live in a small _____ in Manitoba.

Week 27: The Two Sounds Made By 'oo'

Objective: To make students aware that the vowel pair **'oo'** makes two different sounds in words.

Day 1: Introduce the **long 'oo'** vowel sound with the following sentence. It could be spoken or written on a chart. **Sentence:** Goofy Goose and his troop of geese loved to swoop over the roof of a school honking loudly on their way south. Read the sentence with the students. Discuss the words that have the long 'oo' vowel pair and underline each one. Explain to the students that the vowel pair 'oo' in some words has a long vowel sound. On the same chart record the following sentence. **Sentence:** The scared little lamb stood still while the farmer took all of the wool from its body and then shook like a leaf. Underline the words in the sentence that have the **short 'oo'** vowel sound. Discuss the sounds that 'oo' makes in some words. Explain that the long 'oo' double vowel can be heard at the beginning, the middle or at the end of a word. **Examples:** ooze, noon, zoo. The short 'oo' double vowel is usually heard inside a word. **Examples:** shook, stood, book

Picture Key: Row 1: book, kangaroo, cookie, igloo Row 2: tooth, brook, wool, balloon Row 3: football, roof, moose, wood

Activity Worksheet: Page 164 Students will classify the vowel pair 'oo' as the long or short sound. **Answer Key:** Row 1: short oo; long oo; short oo; long oo Row 2: long oo, short oo, short oo, long oo Row 3: short oo, long oo, long oo, short oo

Day 2: Review the **long** and **short 'oo'** vowel combinations. Record the following words on a chart and have the students locate the one that matches the following meanings. **Words:** 1. hood 2. stool 3. hoop 4. cook 5. hoot 6. snooze 7. hook 8. hoof 9. stood 10. noon **Clues given by the teacher:** 1. used for fishing (hook) 2. a seat with no back or arms (stool) 3. a time during the day (noon) 4. a horse's foot (hoof) 5. to have a little sleep (snooze) 6. the sound an owl makes (hoot) 7. a person who prepares food (cook) 8. a round, plastic circle used for playing (hoop) 9. the opposite to sat (stood) 10. a kind of hat (hood)

Picture Key: Row 1: tooth, wool, stool, hood Row 2: brook, igloo, crook, roof

Activity Worksheet: Page 165 The students are to spell and record the word for each picture and then use each word to complete a sentence. **Answer Key: A.** Pictures - Row 1: tooth, wool, stool, hood Row 2: brook, igloo, crook, roof **B.** Sentences: 1. igloo 2. roof 3. tooth 4. stool 5. brook 6. hood 7. crook 8. wool

Day 3: Discuss the long and short sounds made by the vowel combination '**oo**.' On a chart record the following words with the missing vowel combinations. Have the students state which vowel combination is missing. Is it the long or short 'oo.' Have them explain why. 1. b _ _ k (short 'oo' found only inside a word) 2. pool (long oo found inside, at the beginning or end of a word 3. broom (long oo, found inside a word) 4. wood (short oo, found inside a word) 5. boo (long oo, found at the end of a word) 6. moose (long oo, found inside a word) 7. shook (short oo, found inside a word) 8. cookie (short o, found inside a word)

Picture Key: Row 1: school, wood, wool, rooster Row 2: spool, hoof, hoop, brook

Activity Worksheet: Page 166 The students are to classify the sound that 'oo' makes in each picture as hard or soft 'oo.' They are to use the words in the Word Box to complete the sentences. **Answer Key:** Pictures: Row 1: long oo, short oo, short oo, long oo Row 2: long oo, long oo, long oo, short oo Sentences: 1.wood 2. rooster 3. spool 4. hoof 5. brook 6. hoop 7. school 8. wool

Day 4: Review the vowel digraphs '**oo, oa, ai, oe,** and **ou**. Record the following incomplete words on a chart and their missing sounds. **Sounds:** oa, oo, oi, oe, ou **Words:** 1. g _ _ d 2. s _ _ _ th 3. b _ _ _ l 4. t _ _ _ 5. fl _ _ _ t 6. fl _ _ _ r 7. h _ _ _ t 8. _ _ ch 9. j _ _ _ n 10. f _ _ t The students are to complete the words with the vowel combinations.

Picture Key: Row 1: book, boat, couch, point Row 2: toes, balloon, mouse, igloo Row 3: coin, hound, spoon, cookie

Activity Worksheet: Page 167 The students are to complete each picture word with the correct vowel combination. The meanings are to be completed with the picture words. **Answer Key**: Pictures - Row 1: b<u>oo</u>k, b<u>oa</u>t, c<u>ou</u>ch, p<u>oi</u>nt Row 2: t<u>oe</u>s, ball<u>oo</u>n, m<u>ou</u>se, igl<u>oo</u> Row 3: c<u>oi</u>n, h<u>ou</u>nd, spoon, cookie **B.** The meanings are to be matched to the picture words. 1. boat 2. balloon 3. coin 4. couch 5. toes 6. hound 7. spoon 8. mouse 9. igloo 10. cookie 11. point 12. book

Day 5: A. Auditory Test on the Vowel Combinations long 'oo' and short 'oo.' Page 168 The students are to circle the 'oo' sound heard in each word spoken by the teacher. Words: 1. poor 2. soot 3. loop 4. kangaroo 5. foot 6. shook 7. balloon 8. hook **Answer Key:** 1. long oo 2. short oo 3. long oo 4. long oo 5. short oo 6. short oo 7. long oo 8. short oo

B. Visual Discrimination Test on the Vowel Combinations long 'oo and short 'oo.' The students are to complete each sentence with a word from the Word Box. **Answer Key:** 1. foot 2. bloom 3. hoot 4. shampoo 5. tool 6. shook 7. stood 8. moose

Name: _____   Day 1 | Week 28

What sounds can 'oo' make?

Did you know that the vowel pair 'oo' has **two** sounds. One is **long** and one is **short**.

In some words it makes the **long** 'oo' sound at the **beginning**, in the **middle** or at the **end** of a word. **Examples:** ooze, room, zoo

In some words the vowel pair 'oo' has a short sound and is found **inside** a word. **Examples:** book, good, wood

Which vowel sound do you hear in each picture?

On the line under each picture print **long** 'oo' or **short** 'oo.'

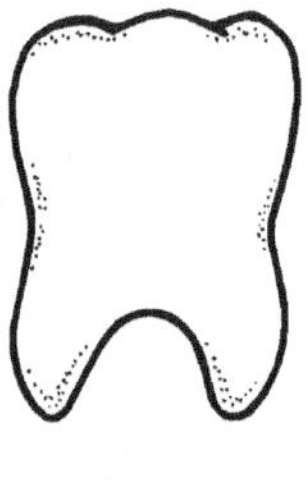

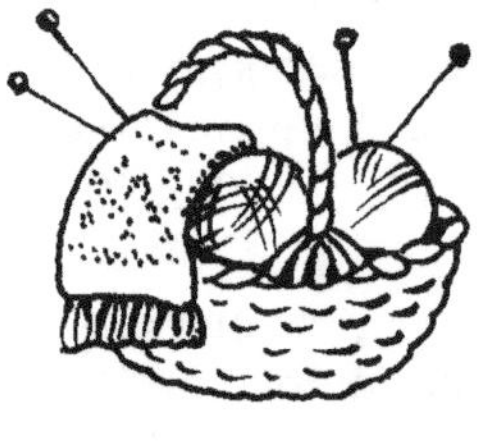

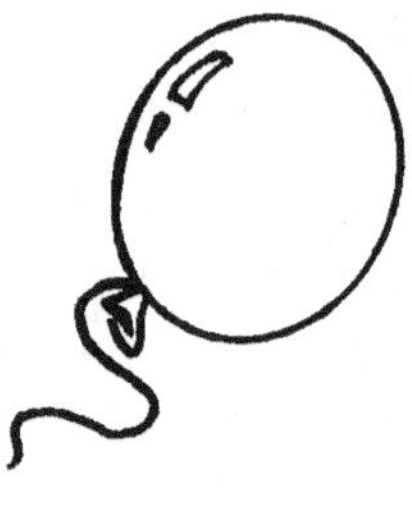

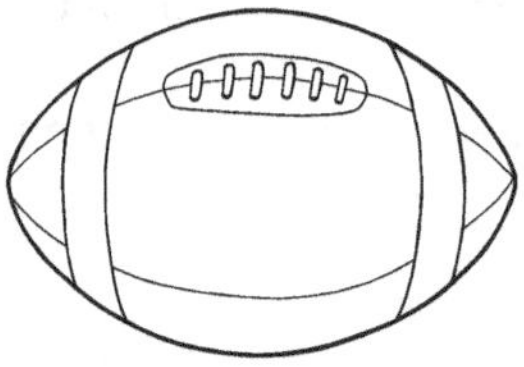

Name: _____   Day 2 | Week 28

The vowel sound 'oo' makes the **long** sound at the **beginning**, **middle**, and **end** of a word.

 Examples: ooze, room, boo

The vowel sound 'oo' can also make a **short sound** in the **middle** of a word.

 Examples: wood, good, hood

A. Print the word for each picture on the line.

B. Print the words that you made in the sentences.

1. An _____ is a house made out of blocks of ice and snow.

2. The kite landed on the _____ of a big house.

3. I lost my first baby _____ when I bit into an apple.

4. I had to use a _____ to reach the top shelf.

5. In the spring, the _____ near our house has lots of water.

6. In a fairy tale a little girl wore a cape with a _____

7. A _____ is someone who steals things.

8. _____ is made from the curly, white hair on sheep.

Name: _____   Day 3 | Week 27

Remember the vowel sound 'oo' makes **two** different sounds.

Which 'oo' sound do you hear in each of the following pictures?

Is it the **long** or **short** 'oo' sound?

A. Circle the sound made by the vowel pair 'oo' in each picture.

 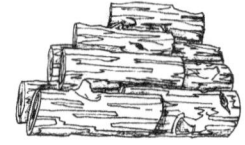  

long oo   short oo   long oo   short oo   long oo   short oo   long oo   short oo

  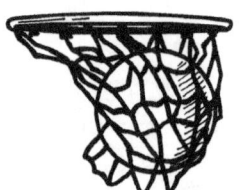 

long oo   short oo   long oo   short oo   long oo   short oo   long oo   short oo

B. Use the following words in the sentences.

school   wood   wool   rooster   spool   hoof   hoop   brook

1. How much _____ will you need to make a fire?

2. The _____ sat on the post and crowed loudly in the morning.

3. The _____ of thread rolled under the chair.

4. The horse lost the shoe from its back _____.

5. The little _____ zig-zagged across the field to the pond.

6. The boy threw the basketball into the _____.

7. At _____ children learn how to read and print letters.

8. The lady spun the _____ into yarn on a spinning wheel.

Name: _____   Day 4 | Week 27

How well do you know the other double vowel sounds found in words.

Double Vowels oo, oa, oi, oe, oa

A. Use these double vowels to complete the picture words.

Is it 'oo, oa, oi, oe, oa?

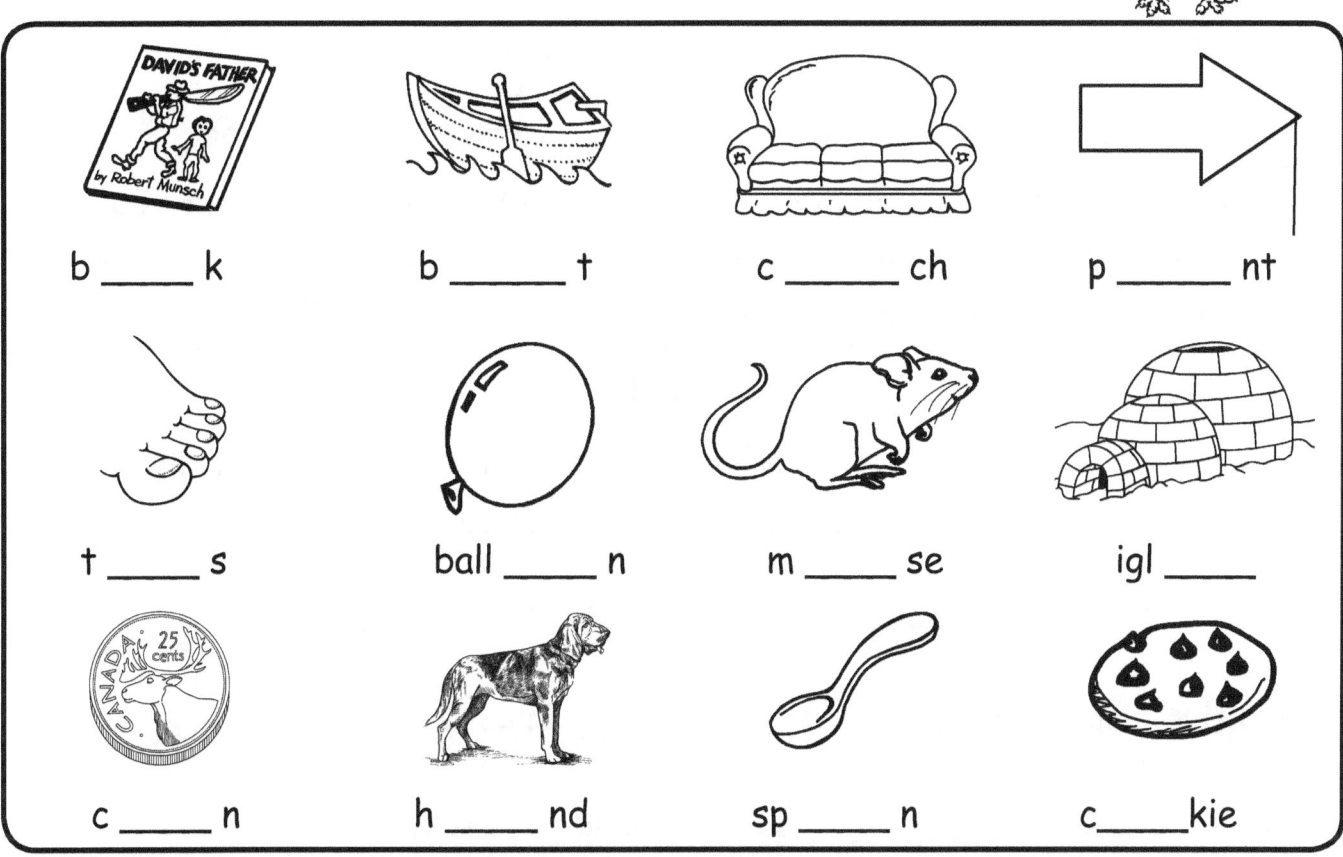

b ___ k   b ___ t   c ___ ch   p ___ nt

t ___ s   ball ___ n   m ___ se   igl ___

c ___ n   h ___ nd   sp ___ n   c ___ kie

B. Match the picture words to their meanings.

1. used on a lake _____   7. used to stir food _____

2. floats in the air _____   8. hides inside a house _____

3. a piece of money _____   9. made of ice and snow _____

4. a place to sit _____   10. a sweet treat _____

5. one foot has five _____   11. your finger does it _____

6. a hunting dog _____   12. something to read _____

Name: _____   Day 5 | Week 27

A. Auditory Test on the Vowel Combinations Long 'oo' and Short 'oo'

1. long oo short oo	2. long oo short oo	3. long oo short oo	4. long oo short oo
5. long oo short oo	6. long oo short oo	7. long oo short oo	8. long oo short oo

B. Visual Discrimination Test on the long 'oo' and short 'oo'

Word Box

moose   stood   foot   bloom   shook   hoot   tool   shampoo

1. I cut my _____ on a piece of glass.

2. In the summer many flowers _____ in gardens.

3. I heard an owl _____ softly during the night.

4. We use _____ to make our hair shiny and clean.

5. A hammer is a _____ used to pound nails into wood.

6. Our dog _____ water all over us after it had a bath.

7. At the hockey game everyone _____ to sing O Canada.

8. The _____ stood in the lake and ate plants growing in it.

Week 28: Silent Consonants 'k, w, l, b'

Objective: To introduce the silent consonants seen but not heard in certain words.

Day 1: On a chart record the following words: kite, walk, kind, sock, keep. Have the students read the words aloud. What sound do you see and hear in all of the words? (initial consonant 'k') Where is the sound located in the words? (at the beginning or at the end of a word.) Record the following words on the chart: knee, know, knew, kneel, knock. Have the students say each word. Discuss how these words are different than the first group read. The words all begin with 'k' but its sound is silent. The sound that you hear is the one that the letter 'n' makes. What will you do if you come to a word that begins with the letters 'kn' and you don't know what it says? Use the sound that 'n' makes to figure out the word.

Picture Key: Row 1: king, knee, kite, knit Row 2: knife, kitten, knuckle, key

Activity Worksheet: Page 170 The students will record the sound 'k' or 'kn' to complete the word under each picture. The words are then to be matched to their meanings. **Answer Key:** Pictures - Row 1: k, kn, k, kn Row 2: kn, k, kn, k Meanings: 1. king 2. knuckle 3. knife 4. kitten 5. kite 6. key 7. knee 8. knit

Day 2: On a chart record the following words: wind, water, wish, week. Have the students read the words aloud. What sound do you see and hear in all of the words? (initial consonant 'w') Where is the sound located in each word. (at the beginning) Record the following words on the chart: write, wrap, wrong, wrist. Have the students say each word. Discuss how these words are different from the first group read. The words all begin with a 'w' followed by an 'r.' Which sound do you hear at the beginning of each word? (r) Which sound is silent? (w) What will you do if you come to a word that begins with 'wr' and you do not know what it says? (Use the sound that the 'r' makes to figure out the word.)

Picture Key: Row 1: well, wrist, wall, wreath Row 2: wind, wrench, web, write

Activity Worksheet: Page 171 The students will record 'w' or 'wr' to complete the word for each picture. **Answer Key:** Pictures: Row 1: w, wr, w, wr Row 2: w, wr, w, wr Sentences: 1. write 2. wrist 3. well 4. wrench 5. web 6. blew 7. wall 8. wreath

Day 3: Record the following words on a chart. **Words:** belt, fell, girl, small Have the students say each word. What sound do you hear and see in all of the words? (the letter 'l') Record the following words on the chart: calf, talk, yolk, should. Have the students say each word. What consonant is seen in every word? (l) Can you hear its sound inside each word? (No, it is silent.) Listen to the following words. If the word that I say has the sound that 'l' makes raise your hands. If you cannot hear its sound sit quietly. **Words**: would, melt, chalk, balloon, calm, helmet, salmon, melon

Picture Key: Row 1: palm, ball, yolk, whale Row 2: pail, chalk, pencil, calf

Activity Worksheet: Page 172 **A.** Students will listen for the sound that 'l' makes in each word and decide if it is heard or silent. **A. Pictures:** Row 1: No, Yes, No, Yes Row 2: Yes, No, Yes, No **B: Words:** 1. calf 2. palm 3. whale 4. yolk 5. chalk 6. ball 7. pail 8. pencil

Day 4: Record the following words on a chart. **Words:** tub, bug, cabin, bulb. Have the students read the words. Which consonant do you see in every word? (b) What sound does the 'Bb' make? (buh) Record these words on the chart. **Words:** comb, climb, crumb, lamb. Have the students read the words or say them after you. What letter is at the end of each word? (b) Can you hear the letter 'b?' (No) At the end of some words the letter 'b' is silent. Each word that I am going to say has the letter 'b' in it. Sometimes you can hear it and sometimes it is silent and you wouldn't know there was one. Raise your hand if you cannot hear the letter 'b.' **Words:** butter, lamb, comb, tub, boot, climb, rub, limb

Picture Key: Row 1: tub, thumb, limb, bib Row 2: cab, lamb, comb, web

Activity Worksheet: Page 173 **Answer Key:** Pictures: The students are to circle the words in which they can hear the sound that 'b' makes and underline the words in which the 'b' is silent. Sentences: The students are to complete each word with a picture word. **Answer Key:** Picture Words Underlined: tub, bib, cab, web Picture Words Circled: thumb, limb, lamb, comb **B:** Sentences: 1. web 2. lamb 3. thumb 4. tub 5. comb 6. bib 7. cab 8. limb

Day 5: A. Auditory Test on the sounds made by k, kn, w, wr, b, mb, l, silent l. Page 174 **Instructions:** In each box there are two words. Read the words in Box 1. Have the students circle the word that has a silent 'k.' Continue in the same manner. 2. silent w 3. loud b 4. loud l 5. silent b 6. loud w 7. silent l 8. loud k **Answer Key:** 1. know 2. write 3. tub 4. pail 5. comb 6. well 7. chalk 8. kite

B. Visual Discrimination Test on Words with k, kn, w, wr, b, mb, l, silent l: The students are to choose a word from the Word Box to complete each sentence. Answer Key: 1. wreathe 2. talk 3. plumber 4. climb 5. half 6. knee 7. knife 8. knob

Name: _____ Day 1 | Week 28

In some words the letter 'k' stands **alone** at the beginning of a word.

Examples: kill, kid, kind

In other words the letter 'k' is followed by the letter 'n' who does all the talking.

Examples: knee, knit, knew, know

Which sound do you hear at the beginning of each picture? Is it 'k' or 'kn?'

A. Print the correct sound on the line in each picture word.

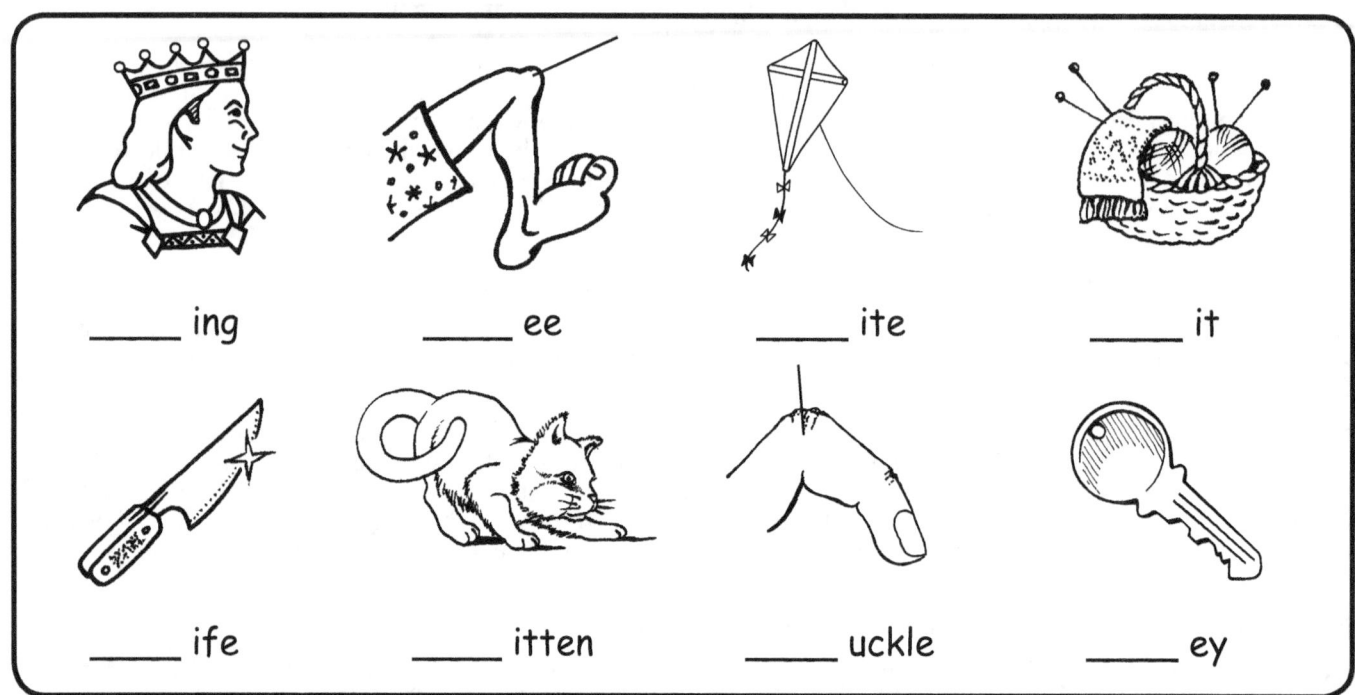

____ ing   ____ ee   ____ ite   ____ it

____ ife   ____ itten   ____ uckle   ____ ey

B. Print the name of the correct picture word beside its meaning.

1. a man who wears a crown _____

2. part of your finger that bends _____

3. used to cut things into pieces _____

4. a furry baby animal _____

5. something you can fly in the air _____

6. used to open things that are locked _____

7. part of your leg that can bend _____

8. to make things with wool _____

Name: _____   Day 2 | Week 28

In some words the letter 'w' stands alone at the **beginning** of a word.

Examples: water, well, wig, wish

In other words the letter 'w' is followed by the letter 'r' who does all the talking.

Examples: wrap, wrong, write, wring

Which sound do you hear at the beginning of each picture. Is it 'w' or 'wr?'

A. Print the correct sound on the line in each picture word.

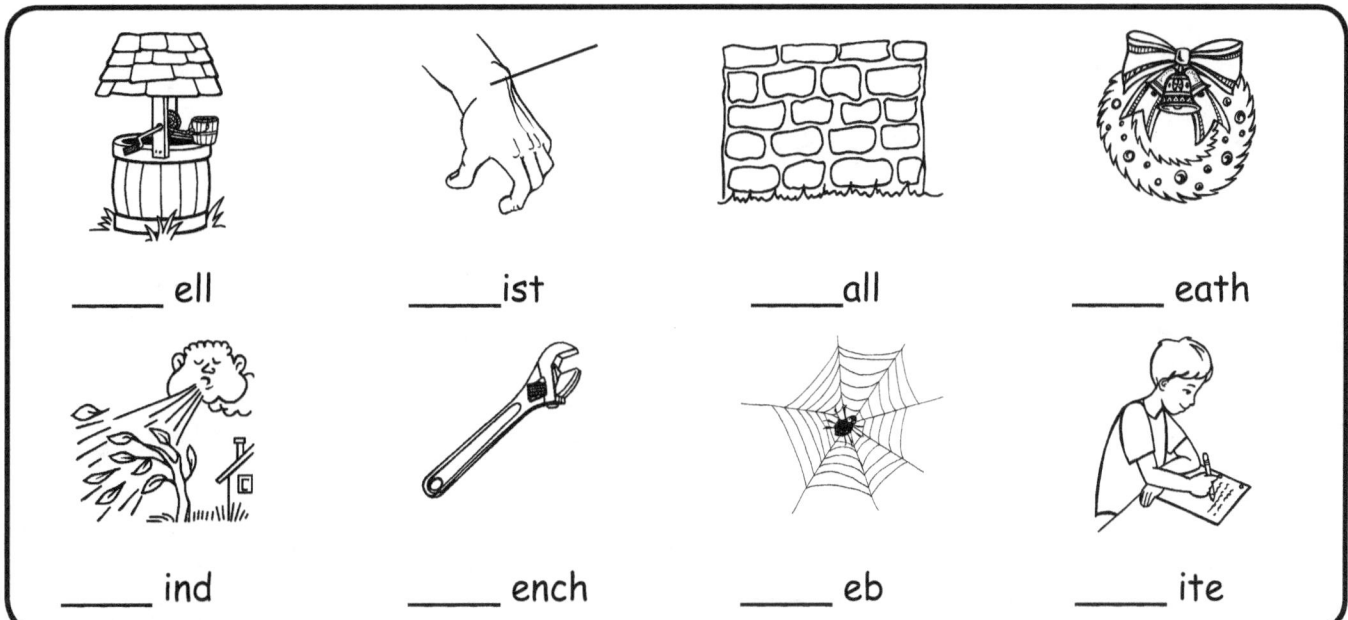

____ ell   ____ ist   ____ all   ____ eath

____ ind   ____ ench   ____ eb   ____ ite

B. Complete each sentence with a picture word.

1. I _____ with my left hand.

2. Your _____ joins your hand to your arm.

3. I went to a _____ to get a pail of water.

4. A _____ is a kind of tool.

5. The spider sat in its _____ waiting for a bug to come in.

6. The wind _____ the leaves on the tall tree.

7. The horse jumped over the stone _____ and ran away.

8. A _____ is often hung on a door of a house at Christmas.

Name: _____   Day 3 | Week 28

In most words the letter 'l' shouts out its own sound.

Examples: land, pole, nail

In some words the letter 'l' is silent. The silent 'l' is found **inside** words.

Examples: walk, could, calm

A. Can you hear the letter 'l' in each picture? Print '**yes**' or '**no**' on the line beside each word.

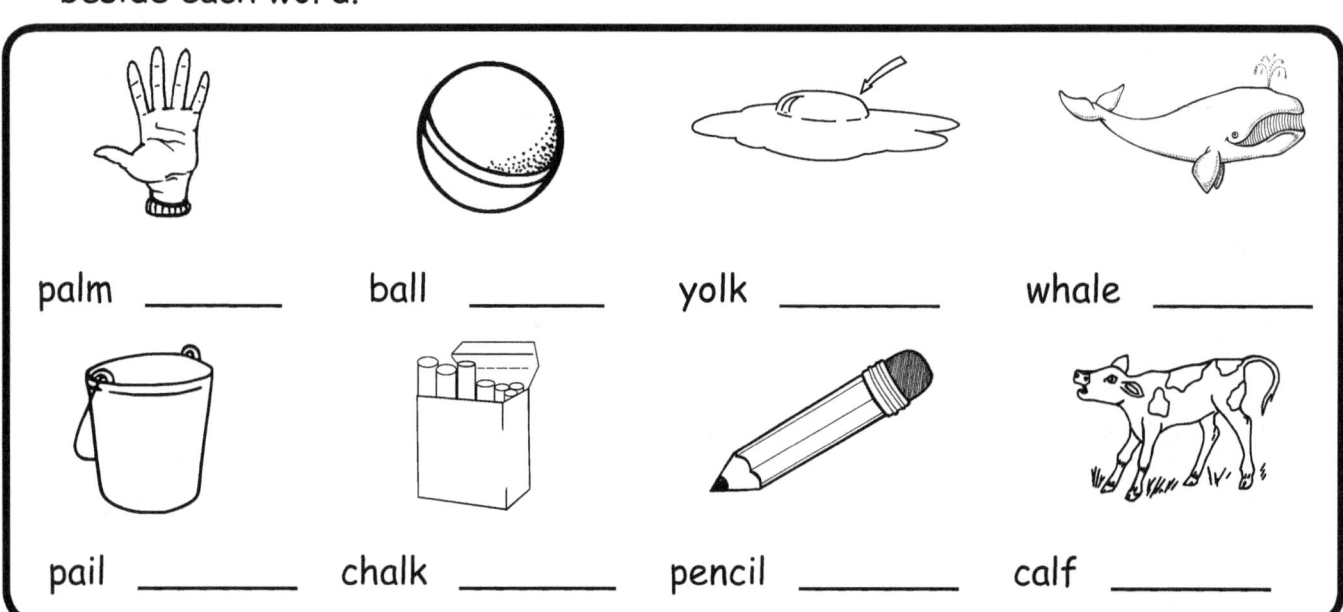

palm _____   ball _____   yolk _____   whale _____

pail _____   chalk _____   pencil _____   calf _____

B. Use the words under the pictures to match the meanings below.

1. a baby farm animal _____
2. part of your hand _____
3. a large ocean animal _____
4. the yellow part of an egg _____
5. used to write on a sidewalk _____
6. used to play kinds of games _____
7. used to carry water _____
8. used to print on paper _____

Name: _____   Day 4 | Week 28

In most words the letter 'b' shouts out its own sound.

Examples: big, cabin, tub

In some words it hides and doesn't make any sound when it follows the letter 'm'.

Examples: lamb, comb, thumb

A. **Circle** the word in each box if you hear the letter 'b' make a **sound**.
   Underline the word in each box if the letter 'b' is **silent**.

B. Use each picture word to complete a sentence below.

1. A spider makes a _____ to trap bugs.

2. The little _____ followed Mary to school one day.

3. On each of your hands you have four fingers and a _____.

4. We gave our dog a bath in the big _____.

5. Did you _____ your hair this morning?

6. The baby wore a _____ around its neck.

7. We went to the airport in a taxi _____.

8. The wind broke a tree _____ and it fell on the ground.

SSR1141 ISBN: 9781771586870   173   © On The Mark Press

Name: _____ Day 5 | Week 28

A. Auditory Test on 'k, kn, w, wr, b, mb, l, silent l

1. kite know	2. water write	3. tub comb	4. pail talk
5. cub comb	6. wrap well	7. chalk tail	8. knee kite

B. Visual Discrimination Test on words with 'k, kn, w, wr, b, mb, l, silent l

Complete each sentence with a word from the Word Box.

> knife   wreathe   talk   plumber   climb   half   knee   knob

1. We hung a _____ on our front door at Christmas.

2. Do not _____ while you are working on a test.

3. The _____ fixed the broken tap in the bathroom.

4. I want to _____ to the top of the hill.

5. I gave _____ of my sandwich to my friend.

6. My brother fell on the sidewalk and hurt his _____

7. A _____ is used to cut food into smaller pieces.

8. Turn the door _____ to open the door.

Week 29: **Contractions**

Objective: To familiarize and make students aware that sometimes two words are shortened to one word and an apostrophe takes the place of the missing letters.

Day 1: Introduce contractions belonging to the **'will'** family. On a chart, record the following pairs of words in a column down it: 1. I will 2. you will 3. she will 4. he will 5. they will 6. we will. Have the students read the words aloud. Tell them that each group of words can be shortened to one word and have the same meaning. Beside each word record its contraction: 1. I'll 2. you'll 3. she'll 4. he'll 5. they'll 6. we'll. Discuss the contractions. What has happened to each pair of words? (It has been shortened to one word.) Is there anything missing from each pair of words? (two letters) What has been placed where the two letters once sat? (an apostrophe or a funny mark) Explain that two words that have been shortened to one word are called a '**contraction**.' An '**apostrophe**' is placed where the two letters are missing.

Activity Worksheet: Page 176 **A.** The students will record the contraction for each pair of words. **B.** Use the contractions to complete the sentences. **Answer Key: A.** 1. I'll 2. we'll 3. she'll 4. he'll 5. you'll 6. they'll **B.** 1. I'll 2. He'll 3. We'll 4. She'll 5. They'll 6. You'll

Day 2: Introduce the '**not**' family of contractions. Record the following contractions across the top of the chart: can't, couldn't, weren't, don't, didn't, aren't, isn't, won't. Record the following pairs of words in a column down it: 1. can not 2. could not 3. did not 4. are not 5. were not 6. is not 7. will not 8. do not Have the students match each contraction to its two words. Which letters is the apostrophe replacing in each group of words? (no)

Activity Worksheet: Page 177 **A.** The students are to match the contraction to its two words. **B.** Contractions in the Word Box are to be used to complete the sentences. **Answer Key: A** - 1. couldn't 2. aren't 3. didn't 4. weren't 5. don't 6. won't 7. isn't 8. can't **B** - 1. Don't 2. won't 3. can't 4. couldn't 5. didn't 6. aren't 7. isn't 8. weren't

Day 3: Introduce the contractions in which 'is' or 'have' have been shortened. Record the following words on a chart: he is, she is, it is, what is, that is, who is, there is, here is. How do you think the contraction for these pairs of words would be written? Have the students give suggestions. When one of them gives the correct answer record the contraction beside each pair of words. The first word of each group will have an 'apostrophe' and 's' added. Record the following words on the chart: I have, you have, we have, they have. Beside each word record the contraction: I've, you've, we've, they've. Discuss how each pair of words was made into a contraction. (The 'ha' of 'have' was removed and an apostrophe put in its place making the two words into one word.

Activity Worksheet: Page 178 **A.** Students are to match each contraction to its meaning. **B.** Students are to complete each sentence with the correct contraction. **Answer Key: A.** 1. here's 2. I've 3. what's 4. that's 5. she's 6. you've 7. it's 8. he's 9. there's 10. who's 11. they've 12. we've **B.** 1. Here's 2. He's 3. She's 4. It's 5. Who's 6. There's 7. What's 8. You've

Day 4: Discuss the contractions in which 'am, are, us, is, and will' are shortened. Record the following words down a chart. **Words:** I'm, you're, let's, she's, he'll. Beside each contraction record the two words each one represents (I am, you are, let us, she is, he will)

Activity Worksheet: Page 179 **A.** Students will record the two words, that mean the same as each contraction, on the lines at the end of each sentence. **B.** Students will record the contraction that has the same meaning on the lines. **Answer Key: A.** 1. we are 2. let us 3. they are 4. I am 5. you are 6. we will 7. it is 8. she is **B.** 1. we're 2. I'm 3. you'll 4. they're 5. it's 6. you're 7. let's 8. I'll 9. he'll 10. here's

Day 5: Auditory Test on the Meanings of Contractions: Page 180 The students are to circle the contraction in each box that has the same meaning as the two words spoken by the teacher. In Box 1, circle the contraction that means 'will not.' Continue in the same manner for the following boxes. 2. it is 3. you have 4. they will 5. I have 6. do not 7. that is 8. I will **Answer Key:** 1. won't 2. it's 3. you've 4. they'll 5. I've 6. don't 7. that's 8. I'll

Visual Discrimination Test on Words that are Contractions: The students are to record the contraction for the underlined words in each sentence on the empty line provided at the end of each one. **Answer Key:** 1. he'll 2. hasn't 3. can't 4. don't 5. we'll 6. won't 7. I've 8. I'll

Name: _____   Day 1 | Week 29

What is a contraction? Did you know that **two words** can be written in a **shorter** way? These words are called **contractions**.

A **contraction** is a shorter way to write two words. A punctuation mark called an apostrophe (') is placed in the shortened word for its missing letters.

Examples: she will - **she'll**; he will - **he'll**

A. **Match** the contraction in the Word Box to its meaning.

Word Box
you'll   they'll   she'll   we'll   I'll   he'll

1. I will _____
2. we will _____
3. she will _____
4. he will _____
5. you will _____
6. they will _____

B. Record the **contraction** on the line that means the same as the **underlined** words.

1. <u>I will</u> go to the store for you. _____

2. <u>He will</u> take the dog for a walk. _____

3. <u>We will</u> ride on a bus to school. _____

4. <u>She will</u> have a cookie for a snack. _____

5. <u>They will</u> plant a tree in their yard. _____

6. <u>You will</u> get a surprise for your birthday. _____

Name: _____   Day 2 | Week 29

Sometimes the letters in the word '**not**' are shortened to make a **contraction**.

Example: can not can't

What is an apostrophe?

The **apostrophe** (') is used to replace the letters '**no**' in the word '**not**.'

Can't is the short way to print can not.

A. Match the contractions in the Word Box to their meanings.

Word Box
can't couldn't weren't don't didn't aren't isn't won't

1. could not _____   5. do not   _____

2. are not   _____   6. will not _____

3. did not   _____   7. is not   _____

4. were not   _____   8. can not _____

B. Use each contraction from the Word Box to complete each sentence.

1. _____ cross the street before you look both ways.

2. My mother _____ let me go to the show with you tonight.

3. We _____ find a big box to put the bicycle in.

4. The bird _____ pull the worm from its hole.

5. Sam _____ pick up all the toys in the yard.

6. There _____ any candies left in the dish.

7. Playing a trick on someone _____ very nice.

8. We _____ going on a picnic because it was raining.

Name: _____   Day 3 | Week 29

Which contraction is it?

Sometimes the word 'is' or 'have' is shortened to make a contraction.

Examples: he is - **he's**; I have - **I've**

A. Match each contraction in the Word Box to its meaning.

Word Box

| he's | that's | it's | she's | what's | I've |
| you've | we've | they've | who's | there's | here's |

1. here is _____
2. I have _____
3. what is _____
4. that is _____
5. she is _____
6. you have _____

7. it is _____
8. he is _____
9. there is _____
10. who is _____
11. they have _____
12. we have _____

B. Choose a contraction from the Word Box to complete each sentence.

1. _____ a good book to read about racing cars.

2. _____ always late for school.

3. _____ always talking on her cell phone in school.

4. _____ fun to swim in a lake on a hot day.

5. _____ that knocking at the back door.

6. _____ a mouse hiding under the big blue chair.

7. _____ in the big bag that you are carrying?

8. _____ been eating all the cookies in the jar.

Name: _____ Day 4 | Week 29

Sometimes the words '**am**, **are**, **us**, **is** or **will**' are shortened in a **contraction**.

Examples: I'm, they're, let's, here's, you'll

Here are some more contractions.

A. Record the two words, that mean the same as each underlined contraction, on the lines at the end of each sentence.

1. <u>We're</u> going on a picnic today at the beach. _____

2. <u>Let's</u> go to the zoo on a bus. _____

3. "<u>They're</u> my boots!" yelled Tom. _____

4. Tomorrow <u>I'm</u> going to pick strawberries at a farm. _____

5. <u>You're</u> the one who spilled the milk on the floor! _____

6. <u>We'll</u> have to travel by train to get to Alberta. _____

7. <u>It's</u> very cold outside today. _____

8. <u>She's</u> the girl that I saw at school. _____

B. Print the **contraction** for each group of words.

1. we are _____   6. you are _____

2. I am _____   7. let us _____

3. you will _____   8. I will _____

4. they are _____   9. he will _____

5. it is _____   10. here is _____

Name: _____   Day 5 | Week 29

A. Auditory Test on the Meanings and Recognition of Contractions.

1. won't we'll we're	2. she's it's let's	3. you'll you're you've	4. they've they're they'll
5. I'm I've I'll	6. don't won't can't	7. that's that'll they've	8. I'm isn't I'll

B. Visual Discrimination of Contractions and their usage.

Print the contraction for each set of underlined words on the line at the end of each sentence.

1. He will read a story to the class. _____

2. Jan has not missed a day of school this year. _____

3. The lame man can not walk to the park alone. _____

4. Do not play with matches as you may start a fire. _____

5. We will help the sick lady get to her home. _____

6. Mark will not stop calling me names. _____

7. I have two dollars to spend at the store. _____

8. I will help you to learn how to skate. _____

Week 30: Irregular Double Vowels 'oo, ea, oi, oy, ow'

Objective: To inform students that some double vowels make two sounds.

Day 1: Introduce the irregular double vowel '**oo**' as in roo**s**ter. On a chart, record the words 'rooster, shoot, pool, and moon.' Discuss the words: Which double vowel do you see and hear in these four words? (oo) What sound does it make? (the long oo sound) Record the following four words on the chart: wood, look, good, hook. Discuss the sound made by 'oo' in these words. (The 'oo' sound makes the short 'u' sound.) Which sound does the double vowel 'oo' make in these words? Is it 'oo' as in book or 'oo' as in broom. **Words:** stool, shook, good, tool, moon, look, stood, tooth

Picture Key: Row 1: stool, book, hook, broom Row 2: wood, goose, hood, spoon

Activity Worksheet: Page 182 The students are to record the word in the Word Box on the line under each picture. They are to mark the 'oo' sound long ¯ or short ˘. The words are to be used to complete the sentences. **Answer Key: A.** <u>Pictures Words</u> - Row 1: sto̅o̅l, bŏŏk, hŏŏk, bro̅o̅m Row 2: wŏŏd, go̅o̅se, hŏŏd, spo̅o̅n **B.** <u>Sentence Words:</u> 1. spoon 2. stool 3. hook 4. book 5. wood 6. goose 7. hood 8. pool

Day 2: Introduce the irregular double vowel '**ea**' as in 'bread.' On a chart record the following words: head, ready, bread, thread. Discuss the words. Which double vowel pair do you see in each word. (ea) What sound does the 'ea' pair make? (short 'ea' sound) Record the following words on the chart: eat, beat, pea and neat. Discuss the double sound in these words. (It is the 'ea' sound that makes the long 'e' sound. Sometimes it may have the short 'e' sound.) Record the following words on the chart: eat, beat, pea, neat. Discuss the double vowel sounds in these words. (The 'ea' sound makes the long 'e' sound) **Listening Exercise:** Which sound does the double vowel sound 'ea' make in the following words? Is it the long 'e' sound or the short 'e' sound. **Words:** eat, head, lead, dead, neat, feather, kneel, easy.

Picture Key: Row 1: head, peach, thread, peas Row 2: feather, leaf, meat, bread

Activity Worksheet: Page 183 The students will match each word in the Word Box to its picture and print it on the line. The vowel combination 'ea' in each word is to be marked with the long ¯ or short ˘ symbol. The words in the box are then to be used to complete the sentences. **Answer Key: A.** Row 1: short ea, long ea, short ea, long ea Row 2: short ea, long ea, long ea, short ea **B.** Sentences: 1. leaf 2. peach 3. feather 4. thread 5. head 6. meat 7. peas 8. bread

Day 3: Introduce the irregular double vowels '**oi**' and '**oy**.' On a chart record the following words: oil, boil, join. Discuss the words. Which double vowel pair do you see in each one? (oi) What sound do the letters 'oi' make in the words. (long o) Record the following words on the chart: boy, toy, joyful, destroy. Read and discuss the words. What sound do the letters 'oy' make in these words? (short o) **Listening Exercise:** Which sound does each pair of double vowels make in each word? Is it long 'o' or short 'o'? **Words:** voice, coil, annoy, soil, toy, royal, coin, spoil, joy

Activity Worksheet: Page 184 The students are to complete each word with the correct vowel combination. They are also to match a word from the Word Box to each meaning. **Answer Key: A -** 1. oil 2. join 3. boy 4. coin 5. toy 6. joint 7. enjoy 8. point 9. boil 10. joy 11. soil 12. destroy **B.** 1. joyful 2. coin 3. boil 4. toy 5. voice 6. enjoy 7. noise 8. cowboy

Day 4: Introduce the irregular double vowel '**ow**' that has a long 'o' and a short 'o' in words. On a chart list the two groups of words in two columns on it. **List 1:** know, show, blow, crow **List 2:** down, cow, bow, owl Have the students read the words and underline the letters that make the same sound in each list. Discuss the two sounds that 'ow' can make in words. The 'ow' in snow has the long 'o' sound while the 'ow in down has the short 'o' sound. Listen to these words. Raise your hand if you hear the short 'o' sound: row, crown, glow, brown, crowd, yellow, throw, towel, cow

Picture Key: Row 1: snow, crown, clown, crow Row 2: cow, throw, flower, bow

Activity Worksheet: Page 185 The students are to record the name of the sound heard in each picture on the line. They are to complete each sentence with a word from the Word Box. **Answer Key: A.** Row 1: long o, short o, short o, long o Row 2: short o, long o, short o, long o **B.** 1. bow 2. throw 3. snow 4. clown 5. crown 6. crow 7. cow 8. flower

Day 5: A. Auditory Test on the Irregular Double Vowels 'oo, ea, oi, oy, ow. The students are to circle the vowel sound that they hear in each word spoken by the teacher. **Words:** 1. toy 2. powder 3. follow 4. point 5. treat 6. boot 7. boy 8. hook **Answer Key:** 1. oy 2. ow 3. ow 4. oi 5. ea 6. oo 7. oy 8. oo

B. Visual Discrimination Test on Words With the Irregular Double Vowels oo, ea, oi, oy, and ow. Answer Key: 1. voice 2. feather 3. crook 4. sea 5. tooth 6. point 7. town 8. throw 9. enjoy 10. oil

SSR1141 ISBN: 9781771586870 181 © On The Mark Press

Name: _____   Day 1 | Week 30

Do you know that the double vowel 'oo' can make two **different** sounds in words?

It can say the **long oo** sound in the word '**rooster**' and the **short oo** sound in the word '**hook.**'

Examples: Long oo: goose, tooth, pool
Short oo: look, good, shook

A. Record each word in the Word Box on the line under its picture. Mark 'oo' with the ¯ long vowel mark or the ˘ short vowel mark in each word.

Word Box

spoon   hood   goose   wood   broom   hook   book   stool

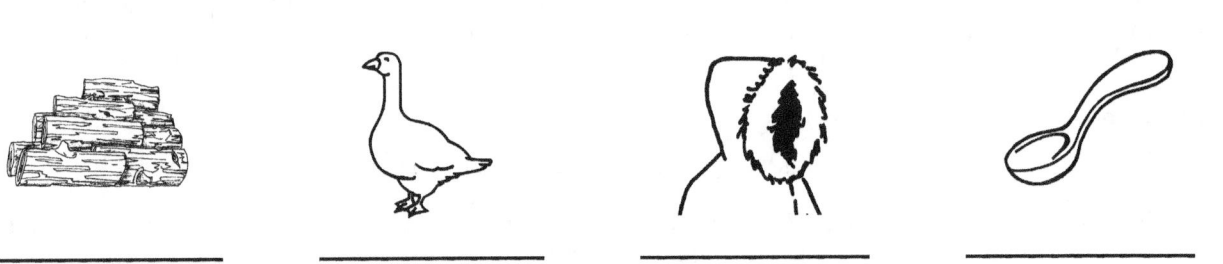

B. Use the words in the Word Box to complete each sentence.
1. The boy used a big _____ to eat his soup.
2. Little Miss Muffet sat on a _____ while she ate her breakfast.
3. Hang your coat on the _____ that your name is under.
4. Which _____ would you like to read.
5. My father put some _____ in the fireplace to make a fire.
6. The little _____ was lost and honked sadly for its flock.
7. My winter coat has a _____ that keeps my head warm
8. I like to jump and play in the _____ in our backyard.

Name: _____ Day 2 | Week 30

The double vowel 'ea' can also make **two** sounds. It can say the **long** 'ea' sound as in the word **leaf** and the **short** 'ea' sound as in the word '**head**'.

Examples: Long 'ea': sea, weak, eat

Short 'ea': head, bread, read

A. Record each word in the Word Box on the line under its picture. Mark the 'ea' sound with the ⁻ **long** mark or the ˘ **short** mark in each word.

Word Box
peach feather peas head thread leaf bread meat

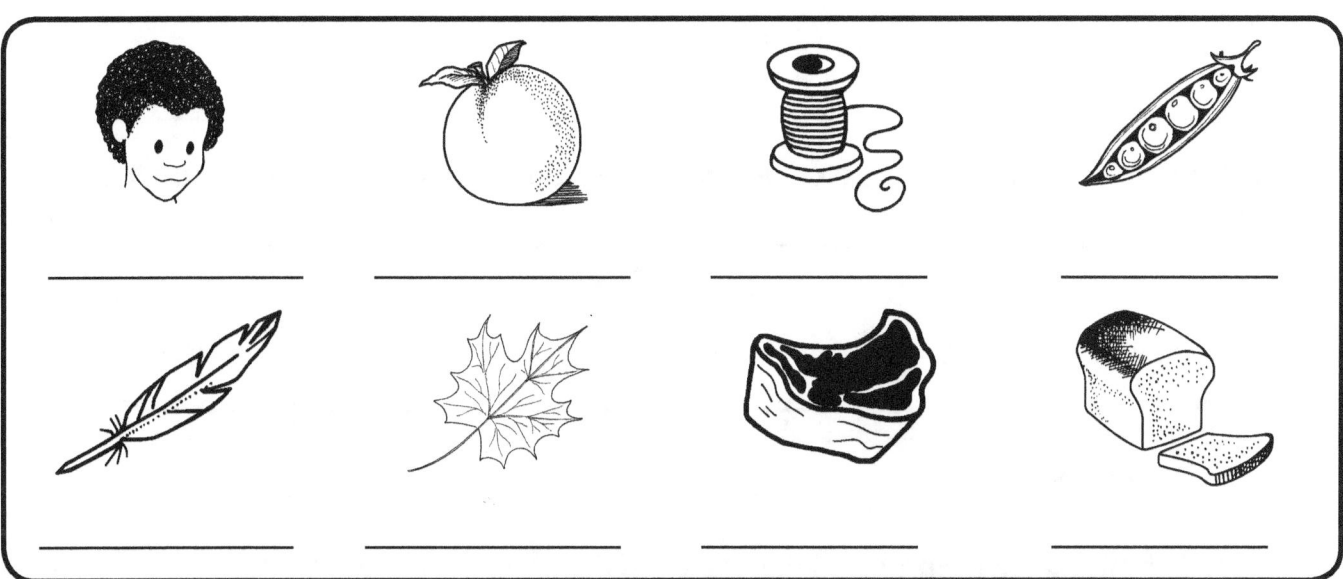

B. Use the words from the Word Box to complete the sentences.

1. The _____ slowly fell from the tree to the ground.

2. A _____ is a yellow fruit that grows on a tree.

3. Many years ago people used a _____ called a quill for a pen.

4. _____ is used to sew clothes together.

5. The boy had a baseball cap on his _____.

6. Which kind of _____ do you want in your sandwich.

7. _____ grow inside a green pod.

8. My mother likes to make and bake her own _____

Name: _____   Day 3 | Week 30

The double vowels 'oi' and 'oy' make the same sound.
Examples: oil, boy
The vowel sound 'oi' is usually found inside a word.
Example: boil
The vowel sound 'oy' is usually found at the end of a word. **Example:** destroy

A. Which sound would you use to complete each word?
   Would you use 'oi' or 'oy.'

1. ____ l   5. t ____   9. b ____ l
2. j ____ n   6. j ____ nt   10. j ____
3. b ____   7. enj ____   11. s ____ l
4. c ____ n   8. p ____ nt   12. destr ____

B. Find a word in the Word Box that matches each meaning. Print it on the line.

Word Box
cowboy   noise   enjoy   voice   boil   toy   coin   joyful

1. to be very happy _____

2. a piece of money _____

3. to cook in very hot water _____

4. something to play with _____

5. used for talking and singing _____

6. you find it fun to do _____

7. a sound heard _____

8. someone who rides a horse _____

Name: _____   Day 4 | Week 30

The letters 'ow' sometimes makes a **long vowel** 'o' sound or it may make a **short vowel** 'o' sound

Examples: snow - long o
cow - short o

A. Which sound do you hear in the pictures? Is it the **long** 'o' or the **short** 'o' sound. **Print** the name of the sound on the line under each picture.

_____   _____   _____   _____

_____   _____   _____   _____

B. Use the words in the Word Box to complete the sentences.

Word Box
crown   crow   throw   bow   clown   flower   cow   snowflakes

1. I tied a pretty pink _____ on my sister's birthday present.
2. How far can you _____ a ball?
3. _____ fell everywhere during the storm last night.
4. The _____ rode on the pony backwards and held onto its tail.
5. The princess wore a _____ of gold with shiny stones.
6. I heard the rooster _____ early this morning.
7. Have you ever tried to milk a _____?
8. I gave my mother a pretty _____ called a rose.

Name: _____   Day 5 | Week 30

A. Auditory Test on the Irregular Double Vowels 'oo, ea, oi, oy, ow'

1. oo ea oi oy ow	5. oo ea oi oy ow
2. oo ea oi oy ow	6. oo ea oi oy ow
3. oo ea oi oy ow	7. oo ea oi oy ow
4. oo ea oi oy ow	8. oo ea oi oy ow

B. Visual Discrimination Test on the Irregular Double Vowels 'oo, ea, oi, oy, ow

Word Box

oil   crook   sea   town   throw   voice   tooth   point   feather   enjoy

1. The girl singing on the stage had a good singing _____.
2. I found a blue _____ on the ground under a tree.
3. A _____ stole some money from a big bank.
4. A _____ is filled with salty water.
5. I lost a _____ and the next morning I found a dollar near my bed.
6. Do not _____ your finger at people.
7. The _____ had a forest fire burning near it.
8. How far did you _____ the ball?
9. Did you _____ watching the hockey game last night?
10. How much _____ will I need to put in the frying pan?

Week 31: Prefixes 're, un, dis'

Objective: To introduce the meanings and usage of the prefixes 're, un, dis.'

Day 1: Record the following words on a chart: do, undo, tie, untie, happy, unhappy. What can you tell us about these words? (They are opposite in meaning.) What makes them opposite in meaning? (the letters 'un' at their beginning) What do you think 'un' means in front of words? (not) The letters 'un' are called a 'prefix' and mean 'not'. It can make words opposite in meaning. It is added to the beginning of a word.

Activity Worksheet: Page 188 The students are to choose the correct form of the word that will complete each sentence. **Answer Key:** 1. unlock 2. dress 3. unhappy 4. unfair 5. tie 6. unopened 7. tidy 8. opened 9. unlocked 10. unwrap

Day 2: Record the following words on a chart. **Words:** read, reread; wind rewind; tell, retell. How does the prefix 're' change the meaning of a word that it has been added to? (It means to do the action again) Record the following words on the chart and have the students use each one in a sentence. Words: rewrap, recover, rewind, undress, unbutton, unfair

Activity Worksheet: Page 189 The students will choose the correct word from the Word Box to complete each sentence. **Answer Key:** 1. rewrite 2. read 3. load 4. rewind 5. rewrap 6. repaint 7. replant 8. retell 9. remake 10. pack

Day 3: Review the prefixes 're' and 'un'. Which prefix can you use with each of the following words. Record the following words on a chart: read, wrap, make, happy, lock, tie, load, open, paint. Have the students print the prefix 're' or 'un' at the beginning of each word and explain its meaning.

Activity Worksheet: Page 190 **A.** The students are to record a prefix at the beginning of each word. **B.** The students will record words from the Word Box to complete each sentence. **Answer Key:** **A.** 1. re 2. un 3. un 4. re 5. un 6. re 7. un 8. re 9. un **B.** 1. unlock 2. unload 3. repair 4. return 5. reload 6. repair 7. untidy 8. unhappy

Day 4: Introduce the prefix '**dis**' which means '**not**' using the following words printed on a chart: disobey, dislike, disappear. What do you think the prefix 'dis' means? (not) What is the opposite word to disobey? (obey) When a word has the prefix 'dis' at its beginning it means 'not' to do the action. On the chart record the following words and have the students tell what each one means: disagree, remake, uncertain, displease, reuse, uncover

Activity Worksheet: Page 191 **A.** The students will choose and record a prefix to place at the beginning of each word. **B.** Students will choose the correct word from the Word Box to complete each sentence. **Answer Key: A.** 1. dis 2. un 3. un 4. dis 5. dis 6. re 7. un 8. dis 9. un 10. re 11. dis 12. re **B.** 1. disobey 2. unfair 3. rewrite 4. unsafe 5. repair 6. unhappy 7. dishonest 8. reread

Day 5: Auditory Test on the Prefixes 're, un, and dis': Page 192 The students are to circle the prefix or the word in each box as directed by the teacher. Box 1: Which prefix means 'to do again' 2: Which prefix means 'not'?
3. Which prefix makes the word an opposite 4. Which word means 'not to do as you are told? 5. Which word means to be messy? 6. Which word means to go back from where you started. 7. Which word means to tell lies. 8. Which word means there is danger. **Answer Key:** 1. re 2. dis 3. un 4. disobey 5. untie 6. return 7. dishonest 8. unsafe

B. Visual Discrimination Test on the Words that begin with the Prefixes "re, dis, and un'. The students will choose words from the Word Box to complete the sentences. **Answer Key**: 1. undo 2. unwrapped 3. disappear 4. untie 5. rewind 6. repaint 7. disobey 8. unbuckle 9. displease 10. redo

Name: _____   Day 1 | Week 31

What is a prefix?

Did you know that a **prefix** can change the meaning of a word.

The prefix '**un**' is sometimes seen at the beginning of a word.

It means '**not**' and can change the **meaning** of the word that it begins.

Examples: happy - unhappy   tie - untie

Choose a word from the Word Box that will complete each sentence.

Word Box
| dress | undress | fair | unfair | tie | untie | lock | unlock | unlocked |
| happy | unhappy | open | opened | wrap | unwrap | tidy | untidy | |

1. Jim had to _____ the door of the school so the children could go in.

2. Cindy will _____ her doll in its new clothes.

3. Bart was _____ when he broke his new toy truck.

4. It is _____ to cheat in a game of cards.

5. I had to _____ up my shoelace before I could run in the race.

6. The gifts under the Christmas tree sat _____ until December 25.

7. Jack's mother told him he must keep his room _____.

8. I _____ all my birthday gifts at my birthday party.

9. The door to the castle was _____ with a big key.

10. I could hardly wait to _____ the big gift under the tree.

Name: _____ Day 2 | Week 31

A **prefix** is a syllable that can change the **meaning** of a word.

'Re' is a **prefix** added to the beginning of a word. It makes the action to **happen again**.

Examples: reread, redo, retell

Choose the word from the Word Box that will complete each sentence.

Word Box

| write | rewrite | read | reread | make | remake | load | reload | plant | replant |
| pack | unpack | wrap | rewrap | paint | repaint | tell | retell | wind | rewind |

1. _____ your messy letter on this clean piece of paper.

2. The boy _____ his story to his class for the first time.

3. The hunter had to _____ his empty gun so he could go hunting.

4. Our hall clock stopped and I had to _____ it.

5. The paper was ripped on Tracey's gift so I had to _____ it.

6. Tony did not like the colour of his room so his father will _____ it.

7. The farmer had to _____ his corn field as the deer had eaten most of the little plants.

8. My grandfather liked to _____ his story about catching a fox many times.

9. My mother made me _____ my bed because I did not do a good job.

10. The old man planned to _____ his old trunks with flags.

Name: _____ Day 3 | Week 31

Re and un are called prefixes.

'**Re**' and '**un**' are called **prefixes**. You may see them at the beginning of words.

'**Re**' means **to do again** and '**un**' means '**not**.'

Examples: redo, undo, recurl, uncurl

A. Record '**re**' or '**un**' at the beginning of the following words.

1. ____ read
2. ____ do
3. ____ happy
4. ____ write
5. ____ fair
6. ____ plant
7. ____ safe
8. ____ write
9. ____ tie

B. Use words from the Word Box to complete the sentences.

Word Box
reload   unlock   unload   return   untidy   repair   untie   unhappy

1. You will have to _____ the treasure chest with this old key.

2. The men will _____ our things at our new house.

3. The man at the garage will _____ my flat tire.

4. Did you _____ the books to the library.

5. The hunter had to _____ his gun so he could shoot at the fox.

6. The man at the store will _____ my broken watch.

7. Billy had to clean up his _____ bedroom before he could play with his friends.

8. I was very _____ that I was late and missed the school bus.

Name: _____ Day 4 | Week 31

The prefix 'dis' is often used to make two words opposite in meaning.

> 'Dis' is prefix that makes words become **opposites**.

Examples: honest - dishonest
colour - discolour
like   - dislike

The prefix '**dis**' means '**not**'.

A. Which **prefix** can you use at the beginning of each word?

Is it '**dis, un,** or **re?**'

Complete each word with the correct **prefix**.

1. ____ colour
2. ____ buckle
3. ____ tie
4. ____ like
5. ____ obey
6. ____ treat
7. ____ fair
8. ____ trust
9. ____ certain
10. ____ tell
11. ____ appoint
12. ____ make

B. Use the words in the **Word Box** to complete the sentences.

Word Box
reread   unhappy   unsafe   disobey   unfair   rewrite   repair   dishonest

1. It is wrong to _____ the laws of Canada.
2. It is _____ not to pay the man for his work.
3. Billy had to _____ his story to correct all of his spelling mistakes.
4. It is _____ to walk or skate on the ice of lakes and rivers in the spring.
5. We had to call the plumber to _____ the broken tap.
6. The children were _____ that they were not going on a picnic.
7. People who steal things are called _____.
8. Everyone in the class is to _____ the story called "The Magic Dragon."

Name: _____   Day 5 | Week 31

A. Auditory Test on the Prefixes 'un, dis, and re'

1. re dis un	2. re dis un	3. re dis un	4. dislike disobey displease
5. remake dislike untidy	6. disappear return unpack	7. dislike disobey dishonest	8. untie unpack unsafe

B. Visual Discrimination Test on the Words that begin with the prefixes 're, dis, and un'

Word Box

| unbuckle | displease | redo | repaint | untie |
| unwrapped | disappear | disobey | undo | unsafe |

1. Will you help me _____ the knot in this skipping rope.

2. I _____ the gift that my brother gave me for my birthday.

3. Did you see the rabbit _____ into his hole to be safe.

4. Please _____ the laces in your shoes before you take them off.

5. I had to _____ the wool into a ball.

6. We have to _____ all the outside doors and windows.

7. Do not _____ the stop sign at the corner of a street.

8. You can _____ your seat belt now as the plane has landed

9. The mess on the floor will _____ your mother when she sees it.

10. Your printing is messy and you will have to _____ it.

Week 32: Suffixes 's, es, ed, ing'

Objective: To familiarize students with the rules involved in adding 's, es, ed, and ing' to the ends of root words.

Day 1: Introduce the **suffix 'ing'** using the following words printed on a chart: looking, playing, fishing, walking. Discuss how the words are similar. (They all end with 'ing.') Explain that 'ing' is added to the ends of action words that tell what is happening in the sentence. Introduce the **suffix 's'** using the following words: walks, talks, writes, grows. How are these words the same? (They all end with 's.') The letter 's' is added to the end of action words that tell how something is moving in the sentence. Introduce the **suffix 'ed'** using the following words: talked, played, helped, looked. How are these words the same? (They all end with 'ed.') The letters 'ed' are added to the ends of action words. These action words tell what has happened in the past.

Activity Worksheet: Page 194 **A.** The students will add the suffixes 's, ed, and ing' to each root word. **B.** Students will select a word from the Word Box to complete each sentence. **Answer Key: A.** 1. hunts, hunted, hunting 2. jumps, jumped, jumping 3. stays, stayed, staying 4. starts, started, starting 5. packs, packed, packing **B.** 1. staying 2. dreams 3. missed 4. brushed 5. buzzed 6. walking 7. helps 8. played

Day 2: Introduce the **suffix 's'** and **'es'**. Record the following words on a chart: dogs, cats, mittens, chairs. Discuss the words. How have these words been written? (They mean more than one thing.) What letter was added to each one to make it mean more than one? (s) Record these words on the chart: boxes, dresses, bushes, churches, buzzes. What two letters have been added to the end of each word. (es) How does each word end if it means only one? (The word may end with ss, sh, ch, x, z.) Record the following words on the chart: glass, bush, can, peach, door, match, bird, fox, mix. Have the students tell which suffix is to be added to make the word mean more than one.

Picture Key: Row 1: brushes, cats, boxes, dishes Row 2: stars, peaches, glasses, foxes

Activity Worksheet: Page 195 **A.** The students are to record the word that names each picture on the line under it. **Answer Key: A.** Row 1: brushes, cats, boxes, dishes Row 2: stars, peaches, glasses, foxes **B.** The students are to add the letter 's' or 'es' to each word. **Answer Key:** 1. es 2. s 3. es 4. s 5. es 6. es 7. es 8. s 9. es 10. es 11. s 12. es 13. es 14. s 15. es

Day 3: Review the suffixes 's, es, ed, ing'. Discuss when the suffixes are to be added. Record the following sentences on a chart. 1. Billy helps his mother. 2. Billy helped his mother. 3. Billy was helping his mother. The letter **'s'** is added to an action word if it is taking place **'now.'** The letters **'ed'** are added to the action word when the action has **already taken place**. The letters **'ing'** are added to the action word when **the action took place in the past.**

Activity Worksheet: Page 196 The student will circle the correct verb for each sentence and print it on the line in each one. **Answer Key:** 1. walking 2. helped 3. fished 4. passes 5. pack 6. barking 7. hunt 8. roasted 9. wait 10. jump

Day 4: On a chart record the following words: bumping, helping, passing, packing. Have the students read the words and listen for the vowel sound. Is the vowel in each word long or short? (short) Record this group of words on the chart: running, hopping, petting, rubbing. Have the students read the words, underline the root word for each one and tell the vowel sound heard. Draw their attention to what happened when 'ing' was added to the end of each one. (The last consonant was doubled before 'ing' was added. Have the students write a rule for adding 'ing' to a word with a short vowel and a single consonant.
Apply the same strategy to teach adding 'ed' to words with a short vowel and single final consonant.

Activity Worksheet: Page 197 **A.** The students are to add 'ed' and 'ing' to each verb. The words in the Word Box are to be used to complete the sentences. **Answer Key: A.** 1. popped, popping 2. begged, begging 3. trotted, trotting 4. snapped, snapping 5. napped, napping 6. dragged, dragging **B.** 1. dripping 2. wagged 3. jabbing 4. wrapped 5. grinned 6. petted 7. grabbed 8. snapping

Day 5: Auditory Test on the suffixes 'e, es, ed, and ing': Page 198 The students are to circle the word in each box that is not spelled correctly. Which word in Box 1 is not spelled correctly? Circle the word. Is it swiming, jumped, buzzes Box 2. chased, rideing, drops 3. Box 3: ride, rides, rideing Box 4: smileed, smiling, smiles Box 5: whipped, whips, whiping Box 6. brushed, brushs, brushing Box 7. huging, hugged, hugs Box 8. beg, begs, beged Box 9. cleanned, cleans, cleaning Box 10. mix, mixs, mixing **Answer Key:** 1. swiming 2. rideing 3. hoping 4. smileed 5. whiping 6. brushs 7. huging 8. beged 9. cleanned 10. mixs

B. Visual Discrimination Test on Words With Suffixes: The students will print the word in each sentence with the correct suffix while making the necessary changes to the root word. Answer Key: 1. running 2. feeding 3. drives 4. trotted 5. skating 6. planned 7. asked 8. taking 9. hoping 10. fishes

193

Name: _____   Day 1 | Week 32

Some words have the letter '**s, ed,** or **ing**' added to their endings.

These words tell how things **move**, how things **are done** or how things **look**.

Examples: jumped, runs, brushing

A. Add the endings '**s, ed,** and **ing**' to each word. Print them on the lines.

1. hunt   _____   _____   _____
2. jump   _____   _____   _____
3. stay   _____   _____   _____
4. start   _____   _____   _____
5. pack   _____   _____   _____

B. Use the words in the Word Box to complete the sentences.

Word Box
brushed   staying   dreams   missed   played   helps   walking   buzzed

1. I am _____ at my grandmother's house for a week.

2. Every night Billy _____ about eating lots of candies.

3. Peter _____ the bus and was late for school.

4. Laura _____ her hair every night before she went to bed.

5. The bee _____ loudly about the flower garden.

6. I like _____ in the woods on a nice day.

7. Everyone _____ my mother clean the house on Saturday.

8. Megan _____ the piano and everyone in the class sang O Canada.

Name: _____ Day 2 | Week 32

Some words that mean more than one thing have the letter '**s**' added at the **end**.

Words that end with '**x**, **z**, **ss**, **sh**, or **ch**' have the letters '**es**' added to their ends.

Examples: boxes, buzzes, dresses, bushes, bunches

A. Print the name of each picture on the line under it. Use the words in the word box.

Word Box
dishes   peaches   cats   stars   glasses   foxes   boxes   brushes

B. Add '**s**' or '**es**' to each of the words.

1. wish ____
2. kitten ____
3. box ____
4. chick ____
5. witch ____

6. hiss ____
7. beach ____
8. ring ____
9. rush ____
10. buzz ____

11. bee ____
12. guess ____
13. fox ____
14. sock ____
15. match ____

Name: _____   Day 3 | Week 32

Words often have different **endings** added to each one.

Examples: help   helps   help**ed**   help**ing**

Print the word in each group that belongs in each sentence on the line.

1. Brenda likes to go _____ in the woods looking for wild flowers.

    (walk, walks, walked, walking)

2. Andy _____ his dad clean out their dirty garage.

    (help, helps, helped, helping)

3. Danny and his brother _____ in a creek behind their barn.

    (fish, fishes, fished, fishing)

4. Every day that truck _____ my house and honks it horn.

    (pass, passes, passed, passing)

5. We will _____ a good lunch for the picnic at the beach on Sunday.

    (pack, packs, packed, packing)

6. The dog in the backyard is _____ at some birds.

    (bark, barks barking, barked)

7. Mr. Black went to _____ for rabbits in the woods.

    (hunt, hunts, hunted, hunting)

8. Lisa _____ hotdogs for supper over a fire when we went camping.

    (roast, roasts, roasted, roasting)

9. The children will _____ for the school bus at the corner.

    (wait, waits, waited, waiting)

10. The girls like to _____ in and out of the skipping rope.

    (jump, jumps, jumped, jumping)

Name: _____ Day 4 | Week 32

Did you know that if a word ends with **one consonant** and has a **short** vowel inside it and you want to add '**ed**' or '**ing**' to the end or it, you must double the consonant.

Examples: stopped hopped dropped
stopping hopping dropping

A. Add '**ed**' and '**ing**' to the words below. Print the words on the lines.

1. pop _____ _____
2. beg _____ _____
3. trot _____ _____
4. snap _____ _____
5. nap _____ _____
6. drag _____ _____

B. Choose the word in the Word Box that will complete each sentence.

Word Box
grabbed jabbing wagged snapping wrapped patting grinned dripping

1. The bathroom tap kept _____ water all day long.

2. The puppy _____ its tail when it saw the boy come home.

3. The bad boy kept _____ me with a very sharp stick.

4. The box that came by mail was _____ in brown paper.

5. I _____ when the happy clown gave me some candy floss.

6. The dog loved being _____ by its owner.

7. Jack _____ the bowl before it fell onto the floor.

8. The big old turtle was _____ at anything that came near it.

Name: _____   Day 5 | Week 32

A. Auditory Test on the Suffixes ' s, es, ed, and ing'

1. swiming jumped buzzed	6. brushed brushs brushing
2. chased rideing drops	7. huging hugged hugs
3. ride rides riding	8. beg begs beged
4. smilied smiling smiles	9. cleanned cleans cleaning
5. whipped whips whiping	10. mix mixs mixed

B. Visual Discrimination Test on Words with Suffixes.

1. The boys were _____ to the park quickly. (run)

2. Jack is _____ his pet rabbits carrots. (feed)

3. Mr. Grey _____ the big yellow school bus. (drive)

4. The old horse _____ down the road pulling a wagon. (trot)

5. I watched the children _____ on the ice of the pond. (skate)

6. My family _____ to take a trip to the Yukon. (plan)

7. Jeff _____ his mom and dad if he could get a puppy. (ask)

8. Mary Ann is _____ her cat for a walk. (take)

9. I was _____ to get a new game to play with for Christmas. (hope)

10. Peter _____ in the creek behind his house. (fish)

Teacher Record:
   Development and Progress of Student Phonetic Skills

Name of Student: _____

Phonetic Skills	Teacher Comments
Initial/Final Consonants	
Long/Short Vowels	
Single/Middle/Final Consonants	
Syllabication in Regular/Compound Words	
Initial Consonant s, l, and r Blends	
Initial/Final Digraphs 'sh, ch, th, wh'	
Vowel Digraphs: 'oa, oe, ow, ue, ew'	
Diphthongs: 'ou, ow, oi, oy'	
Contractions	
Compound Words	
Prefixes/Suffixes	
Word Attack Skills	

Olivia Owl's Phonics Award

This award is presented to _____

for knowing the following phonics skills.

Initial Consonants ____   L Blends ____
Final Consonants ____   R Blends ____
Long Vowels ____   Digraphs: Sh, Ch, Wh, Th ____
Short Vowels ____   Final Consonant Blends ____
S Blends ____   Syllables, Compound Words ____
Vowel Pairs ____   Antonyms, Homonyms, Synonyms ____

www.ingramcontent.com/pod-product-compliance
Lightning Source LLC
Chambersburg PA
CBHW081420230426
43668CB00016B/2293